jB
NIXON

Randolph, Sallie G.

Richard M. Nixon,
President

3/9ᵒ

$13.95

30421

DATE			
NOV 16 1991			

RICHARD M. NIXON, PRESIDENT

Presidential Biography Series

RICHARD M. NIXON, PRESIDENT

Sallie G. Randolph

Walker and Company
New York

First published in the United States of America
in 1989 by Walker Publishing Company, Inc.

Published simultaneously in Canada by Thomas Allen & Son
Canada, Limited, Markham, Ontario

Library of Congress Cataloging-in-Publication Data

Randolph, Sallie G.
   Richard M. Nixon, President / Sallie G. Randolph.
      p.   cm.—(Presidential biography series)
   Incudes index.
   Summary: A biography of the controversial President whose
administration was brought down by the Watergate scandal, but also
reestablished diplomatic ties with China and ended the Vietnam war.
   ISBN 0-8027-6848-2.—ISBN 0-8027-6849-0 (lib. bdg.)
   1. Nixon, Richard M. (Richard Milhous), 1913–   —Juvenile
literature. 2. Presidents—United States—Biography—Juvenile
literature. 3. United States—Politics and government—1945—
-Juvenile literature. [1. Nixon, Richard M. (Richard Milhous),
1913–   . 2. Presidents.] I. Title. II. Series.
E855.R36   1989
973.924'092—dc20
[B]
[92]   89-9080
                                                          CIP
                                                           AC

Printed in the United States of America

10 8 6 4 2 1 3 5 7 9

*For my mother, Alice Ennis Glazier,
and in loving memory of my father,
Richard Montague Glazier.*

Acknowledgments

The author is grateful to President Richard M. Nixon for permission to reproduce many of the prepresidential photographs that illustrate this book. The assistance of many others was invaluable. Special thanks to: Sister Martin Joseph Jones, Archives and Special Collections, E.H. Butler Library, State University College of New York at Buffalo for help in obtaining photographs from the collection of the Buffalo *Courier-Express*; Richard McNeill, Mary Young, and all of the helpful staff at the Nixon Presidential Materials Project of the National Archives and Records Administration for research assistance and photographs; the unfailingly professional and courteous staff members at the presidential libraries of the National Archives and Records Administration who helped provide photographs, including Martin I. Elzy and David Stanhope of the Jimmy Carter Library; Ken Hafeli and Richard L. Holzhausen of the Gerald R. Ford Library; Robert W. Tissing, Jr., and E. Philip Scott of the Lyndon Baines Johnson Library; Allan Goodrich and Donna L. Hanlon of the John Fitzgerald Kennedy Library; Martin M. Teasley and Jim Leyerzapf of the Dwight D. Eisenhower Library; Pauline Testerman, George H. Curtis, and Benedict K. Zobrist of the Harry S. Truman Library; Weirton Steel Corporation in Weirton, WV, for permission to use a photograph provided by the Dwight D. Eisenhower Library; Annette Gernatt and the helpful staff of the Town of Concord Public Library; Joan Asquith and Elizabeth Densmore of the King Memorial Library in Machias, NY; the Town of Tonawanda Public Library; the Buffalo and Erie County Public Library; Jeanne Gardner for her patience, perspective, and wise editiorial counsel; all the members of the Wednesday night "Write People"; and especially Rich Randolph, Sue Harrington, Bob Wieland, Erin Harrington, Eleanor Sullivan, John Randolph, Alice Glazier, Sidney Potmesil, Marge Facklam, and Will Randolph for research help, moral support, information, and advice.

CONTENTS

1

The Darkest Days

The president of the United States walked across the rich blue carpet of the Oval Office and stepped over the gold seal woven into its center. His face had a gray cast, even under the makeup. He summoned up a weak smile as he took his place behind the desk. The American flag pin on his lapel glinted briefly in the fading sunlight.

"Only the crew now is to be in this room during this, only the crew," said Richard M. Nixon.

The president cleared his throat and positioned the papers on his desk. Aides left the room. The camera crew and a lone Secret Service agent remained.

Outside, the nation's capital simmered in the sultry August heat while rumors boiled and the nation waited to see what the embattled president would do.

"Jail to the chief!" chanted angry demonstrators at the White House fence. "Jail to the chief!"

In the Oval Office the television lights blazed, bathing the room in their glare. The red light on the main camera winked on. The president looked up to face it, and the nation.

"This is the thirty-seventh time I have spoken to you from this office where so many decisions have been made that shaped the history of the nation," he began, his voice steady.

Richard Nixon announces his resignation in a nationwide television speech on August 8, 1974.
WHITE HOUSE PHOTO COURTESY *COURIER-EXPRESS* COLLECTION, E.H. BUTLER LIBRARY, STATE UNIVERSITY COLLEGE AT BUFFALO AND BUFFALO AND ERIE COUNTY HISTORICAL SOCIETY.

"Throughout the long and difficult period of Watergate, I have felt it was my duty to persevere, to make every possible effort to complete the term of office to which you elected me. In the past few days, however, it has become evident to me that I no longer have a strong enough base in the Congress to justify continuing that effort."

There was a mechanical quality to his words, and the familiar voice was gravelly with strain. "I have never been a quitter. To leave office before my term is completed is abhorrent to every instinct in my body. But as president, I must put the interest of America first. America needs a full-time president and a full-time Congress, particularly at this time, with problems we face at home and abroad."

The president swallowed before speaking the next fateful words. America waited. "Therefore, I shall resign the presidency, effective at noon tomorrow."

Nixon asked Americans to support the next president and said that he would continue to work for "great causes." He claimed that the world was a safer place because of him. "May God's grace be with you in all the days ahead," he concluded as the camera left his tired image and focused on the presidential seal. The sad, historic moment was over. Richard Nixon, who had been proud of the many "firsts" he had achieved in his lifetime, had established another.

How had he reached this tragic day? Why was he the first to resign as president of the United States? This intelligent, complex man, a product of his times and his fierce ambition, had reached the pinnacle of success and was about to plummet to the depths of defeat. The immediate reason was a scandal called Watergate.

President Nixon tells Vice-President Gerald R. Ford that he is resigning and that Ford will become the new president.
WHITE HOUSE PHOTO COURTESY *COURIER-EXPRESS* COLLECTION, E.H. BUTLER LIBRARY, STATE UNIVERSITY COLLEGE AT BUFFALO AND BUFFALO AND ERIE COUNTY HISTORICAL SOCIETY.

The scandal had grown from what, at first, appeared to be a minor break-in of the Democratic party's Washington headquarters in the plush Watergate office building. Five men had been arrested, men who some reporters noticed might have ties with the White House.

Two dogged *Washington Post* reporters eventually discovered that the Watergate break-in was linked to the Committee to Re-elect the President, nicknamed CREEP, and that legal fees and "hush money" had been paid to the break-in defendants from a secret fund controlled by officials high in the Nixon campaign.

Eventually Watergate was linked to the highest levels of the White House. As the story unfolded, Congress, the press corps, and the public learned that the Watergate break-in was part of a White House security operation that included burglaries, electronic eavesdropping, political spying, and sabotage efforts against the campaigns of several Democratic presidential candidates.

The Senate decided to investigate and appointed a select Watergate committee. Testimony before the committee revealed many of CREEP's illegal practices, but the White House was successful in covering up its own involvement for a while.

Then the committee learned that Nixon, in order to preserve an accurate record of his presidency for history, had arranged for an elaborate taping system in his offices that would record every conversation that took place. The committee tried to obtain the Nixon tapes.

As evidence mounted, the House of Representatives Judiciary Committee began to investigate the possible impeachment of the president. If a president was to be removed from office, the procedure would be for the House of Representatives to vote to impeach, or indict, him. Once impeached and charged with specific offenses, called articles of impeachment, the president would have a trial in the Senate. If, after a full trial on the charges in the articles of impeachment, presided over by the chief justice of the Supreme Court, the Senate voted to find the president guilty, he would be removed from office.

After the existence of the Nixon tapes was revealed, a legal battle for them began, a battle that eventually resulted in the

Richard Nixon hugs his daughter, Julie Nixon Eisenhower, on the eve of his resignation. Throughout the Watergate ordeal, Julie was his staunchest supporter.

WHITE HOUSE PHOTO COURTESY *COURIER-EXPRESS* COLLECTION, E.H. BUTLER LIBRARY, STATE UNIVERSITY COLLEGE AT BUFFALO AND BUFFALO AND ERIE COUNTY HISTORICAL SOCIETY.

release of the tape that proved the president knew about Watergate and had participated in an attempt to cover it up. The scandal resulted in the firings and resignations of most of the top White House staff and sent a number of the president's aides to jail. In the end, Nixon himself became the first president ever to resign.

Americans stayed in front of their television sets the next day as the final drama played out. They watched in grim fascination as President Nixon said an emotional farewell to his staff.

They watched as he and his wife were escorted across the White House lawn to a waiting helicopter by Vice-President Gerald Ford and his wife. They saw bitter defiance in the face of President Nixon as he turned and raised his arms in a familiar gesture of victory.

The helicopter slowly lifted from the White House lawn. Gerald Ford waved farewell, then returned to the White House to be sworn in as the new president. Nixon's helicopter soared into the sad, gray sky.

Inside the helicopter, the silence was broken only by the steady thrum of the whirling blades as they chopped through the dreary clouds.

No one talked—Nixon leaned his head back against the seat and closed his eyes.

"It's so sad," his wife murmured. "It's so sad."

Richard Milhous Nixon has inspired both great loyalty and fierce dislike. He was a president with devoted friends, staunch admirers, and bitter enemies. The blind loyalty he inspired was one of the reasons for the excesses of his administration. And the hatred of his adversaries was one of the reasons those excesses were exposed.

Nixon's harshest critics charge that he had been a compulsive liar from childhood, was emotionally unbalanced, dangerously so in the last days of his presidency, and had been corrupt and ruthless throughout his political career.

Supporters say that the immoderacy of his administration had been brought about by a strong desire to protect the country from forces that divided it. He was a great president,

The Nixons are escorted from the White House by the Fords on Nixon's last morning as president, August 9, 1974.
PHOTO COURTESY NATIONAL ARCHIVES.

they say, who had used commonplace political tactics and sacrificed his presidency for the good of the nation.

Others say Watergate was the culmination of many forces, including the isolation of the president behind his staff, the president's oversimplified "good guys versus bad guys" attitude, his sensitivity to criticism, the rigid White House management style, and the influence of a zealous, inexperienced staff.

For some, Nixon's brilliant accomplishments outweighed the revelations of Watergate. Others said nothing could justify the excesses of his administration.

Richard M. Nixon, the thirty-seventh president of the United States, had overcome long odds and tasted great victory. He had dealt effectively with some of the biggest problems of the times, but his presidency was brought down by a scandal that tore the very fabric of American politics.

Was Nixon a victim of vicious political enemies and an arrogant press? Or was he destroyed by his own ambition and greed for power? Did he follow the long-established, if shady, political traditions of his predecessors or did he willfully subvert the Constitution of the United States?

Only history will tell. Only time will put these questions into perspective. But however history judges him, the story of Richard Milhous Nixon is a fascinating look at the best and the worst of American politics and the presidency.

2

California Childhood

Young Richard Nixon was a dreamer. As a small boy he was fascinated with trains and for many years his ambition was to be a railroad engineer.

Richard and his brothers had an electric train, his mother remembered. "Evenings they would play with it in front of the fireplace. One of the boys was the conductor, another the fireman. Richard was always the engineer."

Richard could see the smoke of the steam locomotives from his childhood home, a house his father had built, in Yorba Linda, California.

"I remember the house at Yorba Linda," said the nurse who attended his birth. "It was a two-story frame affair, situated on a hill overlooking a deep irrigation ditch." He was born in that small house on January 9, 1913, during a time of record cold that threatened the citrus crops of the small farming community outside of Los Angeles.

"He was an unusually big baby, with a crop of black hair and a powerful, ringing voice," the nurse said. Richard was huge by the standards of the day, eleven pounds.

His father threw his arms in the air the next day and danced around the yard in jubilation. "I've got another boy," he shouted.

A Nixon family portrait, taken in 1917 when Richard was four years old, shows Frank and Hannah Nixon with their three oldest children, Harold (left), Donald (center), and Richard (right).
PHOTO COURTESY NATIONAL ARCHIVES.

His mother named him after an English king, Richard the Lion-Hearted, and gave him a middle name, Milhous, after her family. He was the second child, four years younger than his brother, Harold.

His parents were Hannah Milhous Nixon, a gentle Quaker lady of great faith, and Francis Anthony Nixon, called Frank, a stern, hardworking man. Nixon has described them both as deeply religious, devoted to each other, and dedicated to their children.

During Richard's early childhood, Frank Nixon supported his family by taking whatever jobs he could find. The family grew much of their own food in a big vegetable garden and a small fruit orchard. Hannah Nixon made butter and cheese from milk produced by the family cow. Nixon remembers his family life in Yorba Linda as "hard but happy."

When Richard was not quite two, Hannah had another son, Donald. Both parents worked hard to support and raise their three boys. Hannah was a quiet woman, according to the hired man who helped Frank Nixon operate his small lemon grove. "She would hardly ever sit down and eat with us," he said,

This photo of Richard and his older brother, Harold, was taken when Richard was two years old.
PHOTO COURTESY NATIONAL ARCHIVES.

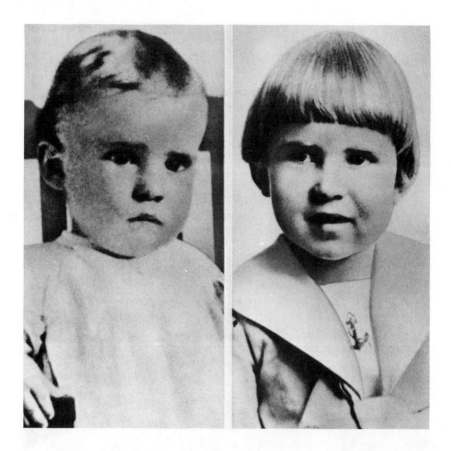

because she was "generally cooking and bringing stuff to the table," before she would take time to eat herself. Frank Nixon helped care for little Richard. "He always sat with his dad at the table, and his dad always fed him," the hired man said.

When Richard was five, another brother was born. The baby, named Arthur after another English king, was a disappointment to Richard. "A tiny baby is not as pretty as a doll," he said. Nevertheless, he watched with fascination how the baby grew.

A few months after the birth of Arthur, Richard's widowed aunt and her two sons came to share the Nixon home. One of the cousins, Floyd, was the same age as Richard's big brother,

These four portraits show Richard Nixon at six months, three years, eighteen years, and as a member of his college football team.
PHOTO COURTESY NATIONAL ARCHIVES.

Harold. Young Dick looked up to the two older boys and tried to hang around with them.

The older boys teased him often and took advantage of his desire to please them and of the competitive nature that young Dick was developing. "We would bet him that he couldn't get up to the house and bring us cookies or a bottle of milk or something and get back to us before we could count to a hundred," Floyd remembers.

"He'd take off on the run, we'd sit there and visit until we saw him coming. Then we'd pick up the count somewhere in the nineties . . . and we'd just get him under the wire at about ninety-seven. He'd get there all puffing, but he'd always win."

When the Nixon boys got in trouble, the reaction of their parents was entirely different. Frank was voluble and hot tempered. He would erupt into anger, shouting and sometimes dishing out a few swats. His punishments were quickly over and forgotten.

"My father was strict," Richard said. "He believed that if you spare the rod you spoil the child."

Hannah didn't believe in violence. "My mother was very firm, but in her whole life I never heard her raise her voice," Richard said. But he dreaded her tongue even more than his father's temper. Although her tone was never sharp, a "talking to" from his mother was an emotional experience.

"Tell her to give me a spanking," Arthur had pleaded one time. "Don't let her talk to me. I just can't stand it, to have her talk to me."

Richard Nixon, in his last speech in the White House, would refer to his mother as a "saint." So did many of the people who knew her as a young woman. Deeply religious, serious, and thrifty, she was willing to sacrifice for the sake of her sons. She wasn't a joyful woman but she was ambitious. "She instilled in the family this seriousness about growing up and being somebody," one family member said.

Frank Nixon was far less restrained. He had strong feelings and wasn't afraid to express them. He loved to argue and often involved his small sons in boisterous discussions. Dinner conversations often became shouting matches until Hannah would interject, "Now hush, all of you."

"You make them hush, and I'll hush," Frank would snap.

"Don would try to outshout Frank," one cousin recalled. "He would just stand up and bellow at him right back, like two bulls." Harold was quick to join in the fray as well. "Their shouting could be heard all through the neighborhood."

Young Dick avoided confrontations with his father by escaping into a world of his own. "I can recall that when we'd want Dick to do something we could never find him," Floyd said. "He

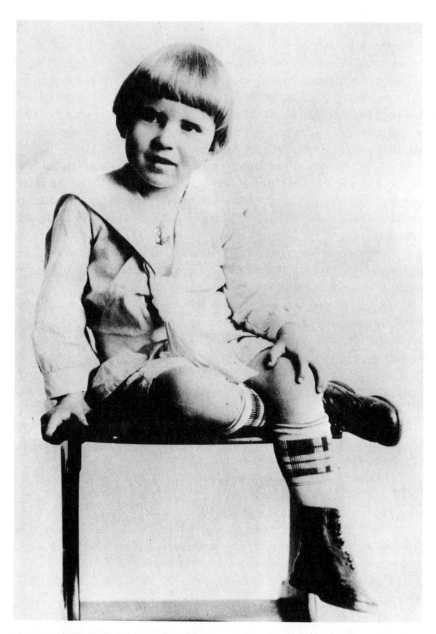

Richard Nixon at three years old.
PHOTO COURTESY NATIONAL ARCHIVES.

was always gone. Dick would always hide out. We got so we'd hunt him."

"I can still see him lying on the lawn, sky-viewing and day-dreaming," remembers his aunt.

Those daydreams would take young Richard far, far away from the crowded house in Yorba Linda. Even at this early stage of his life, Dick Nixon planned to see the world. "I dreamed of the far-off places I wanted to visit someday. I had in me some wanderlust," he said. "Geography was my best subject."

At night, as his three brothers slept in the same room, he would lie awake and listen for the train whistle. When its throaty blast would echo in the quiet country night, his imagination would soar. He called it the sweetest music he had ever heard.

If Richard had been born later, he probably would have wanted to be an astronaut. "If space had been the thing, I would have wanted to go around in a space helmet."

Even as a very little boy, he was acutely curious, always anxious to learn and do well. Richard knew how to read before he began school. His mother had taught him. He was anxious to please, so school was a place where this smart boy could be happy.

He was a serious child. "He wasn't a little boy that you wanted to pick up and hug," his cousin Jessamyn West once said.

Richard was also always neat and meticulously groomed. Even though he went to school barefoot, as did the other children, he wore a clean white shirt with a big black bow tie. "He always looked like his mother scrubbed him from head to toe," his first grade teacher said. "The funny thing is, I can never remember him ever getting dirty."

"He was interested in things way beyond the usual grasp of a boy his age. He was thoughtful and serious," his mother said. "He always carried such a weight," she added. "That's an expression we Quakers use for a person who doesn't take his responsibilities lightly."

Hannah Nixon remembered how hard her son struggled to succeed. "As you know, most boys go through a mischievous period. Then they grow up and think they know all the answers.

The four oldest Nixon brothers play outside their childhood home in Yorba Linda, California, in 1922. Seven-year-old Donald is curled in the tire. In back, from left to right, are Richard (nine), Harold (thirteen), and Arthur (four).
PHOTO COURTESY NATIONAL ARCHIVES.

Well, none of these things happened to Richard. He was very mature even when he was five or six years old."

Richard tried everything with dogged perseverance. He played school-yard baseball and football, even though he was quite clumsy and, considering his birth size, small for his age. He didn't do very well at athletics, but he always went back for more.

He was better at music. "He had a natural ear," his mother said. By the time he was seven he could pick out tunes on the piano, so he started taking piano lessons with his uncle. Later he would be sent to live for a while with an aunt who would give him advanced piano instruction.

And he was even better at his schoolwork. There he impressed everyone with his excellent memory, his fine mind, and his willingness to work hard. His first grade teacher seated him in the back of the classroom because he didn't need supervision. "He absorbed knowledge of every kind like a blotter," she said.

Richard loved to read. His favorite magazine was the *National Geographic*, which he studied from cover to cover every time he visited his aunt, who was a subscriber. In first grade "he read no less than thirty or forty books, maybe more, besides doing all his other work," his teacher said. He did so well that he skipped the second grade.

Church was another important part of Richard's life and it was there that he first learned public speaking. He was encouraged to stand up and speak out before the congregation in the Quaker tradition. At the same time he was discouraged from showing his personal feelings, another side of his Quaker heritage.

Richard was fascinated from an early age with politics, which he discussed frequently with his exuberant, opinionated father. Frank Nixon taught Sunday school and Richard attended his class regularly from the age of five on. The focus of the class was the need to practice Christianity in contemporary politics. Richard "took serious part in the discussions. He expressed opinions. He had a remarkable memory for the things he learned," said one of his classmates.

His father's political views were more enthusiastic than reasoned, but Richard was intrigued by the discussions. He read the newspaper avidly each day. He talked about politics to his elementary school classmates.

When he was eleven, a great scandal broke, the Teapot Dome Scandal. Teapot Dome was the name given to the most famous scandal of the administration of President Warren Harding, the most corrupt of all presidencies, according to most historians. Harding's secretary of the interior, Albert Fall, a cabinet member, arranged for the transfer of valuable government oil reserves to his control. He then sold those reserves at Elk Hills, California, and Teapot Dome, Wyoming, to private oil companies, making an illegal fortune for himself in the process. Fall was eventually convicted of accepting a bribe and was sentenced to prison. Frank Nixon was incensed and railed against the corrupt politicians who had betrayed the public trust. He also denounced the lawyers who defended them for fat fees.

"When I get big," Richard told his mother one day after a new scandalous revelation was spread across the front pages, "I'll be a lawyer they can't bribe."

3

A Young Adult

The trees in Frank Nixon's Yorba Linda lemon grove were mature but never did bear much fruit. Although Richard's family worked hard, it struggled in the shadow of poverty. So, in 1922, when Richard was nine years old, Frank decided to move. He sold the farm and the Nixons moved to Whittier, near Hannah's large Quaker family.

The Milhous clan was prominent in Whittier. Family and church activities dominated life in the small California city. Frank built another house for his family, settled them in, and then worked for two years as a roustabout in the booming oil fields nearby.

When he had saved enough to invest, Frank Nixon established a store and gas station on the main road. The Nixons weren't particularly well-off. But the store provided a living, even if the work was almost nonstop. "They worked us kids to death," Donald Nixon once said. But the hard work brought the family together.

In midsummer of the year Richard was twelve, tragedy darkened the family's life.

This 1927 snapshot shows Richard at age thirteen, left, with Donald.
PHOTO COURTESY NATIONAL ARCHIVES.

"Just a case of indigestion, we thought," Nixon wrote about his little brother, Arthur. "But a week went by and his condition became worse instead of better. He began to become sleepy; he did not want to eat; he wanted to rest and sleep. Several doctors came to see him, but none could see what his trouble was. Finally, my father sent me with my younger brother to the home of an aunt who lived nearby, fearing that we too would become ill. One night my aunt awakened us and told us to get dressed. Arthur was a little worse, she had said."

They went home. "My father met us with tears in his eyes. He did not need to tell us what we knew had happened." The cause of Arthur's death was not certain, but it was probably tubercular meningitis.

"I can still see Richard when he came back," his mother said. "He slipped into a big chair and sat staring into space, silent and dry-eyed in the undemonstrative way in which, because of his choked, deep feeling, he was always to face tragedy."

His mother also noticed another effect. "I think it was Arthur's passing that first stirred within Richard a determination to help make up for our loss by making us very proud of him. Now his need to succeed became even stronger."

Richard threw himself anew into a grueling schedule. He got up early each day to do chores. When he was older he got up at three o'clock in the morning and drove the truck into the Los Angeles farm market to buy produce for the store. He returned home, dumped his load of fruit and vegetables into a big tub, and washed everything carefully.

Next, he would put in a full day at school. After Whittier Elementary School he attended high school in Fullerton for two years, then transferred to Whittier High School for his last two years. He kept up the relentless striving for his excellent grades and discovered a talent for debating. He continued to study piano and took up the violin. Once he won an award for a speech on the United States Constitution. "It is our duty," the young Nixon said, "to protect this precious document, to obey its laws, to hold sacred its mighty principles."

Richard's formula for success was a simple one. "Dick always planned things out," said his brother Don. "He didn't do things accidentally. He had more of Mother's traits than any of us."

"I think of Dick as a 'fighting Quaker,' " his high school principal remembered. "He was a leader in scholastic and student activities, a self-starter."

His debating coach was both proud of his skill and a bit disturbed by it. "He had this ability to kind of slide around an argument instead of meeting it head-on, and he could take any side of a debate," the coach said.

After school he'd return to the store to polish the produce and set up an attractive display. The Nixon market was built from a former church building that had an old bell tower where Dick would retreat. After each long day, he would climb to his hideaway to study and dream. Sometimes the early delivery crews would find him with his light still on after studying all night.

Richard Nixon was a sophomore and orchestra member at Fullerton High School in 1928.
PHOTO COURTESY NATIONAL ARCHIVES.

The loss of his little brother was hard for Richard to accept, especially since it was followed in just a few years by another tragedy. Harold Nixon, the amiable older brother, the only person, some said, who could make Richard laugh, contracted tuberculosis, and the dreadful illness became the center of all the family's efforts.

Harold would stand a better chance in the dry climate of Arizona, his doctors said, so Hannah took him to Tucson, leaving Richard and Donald home with their father to run the store.

She stayed for two years, earning enough money to support Harold by taking in other tuberculosis patients and nursing them. At home, Richard's life degenerated from grueling to Spartan, an endless round of hard work, study, and worry. His mother had been the one to soften Frank's brusque nature. Without her, life at the Nixon home and store was especially hard.

"We all grew up rather fast in those years, those of us who remained at home," Richard said. He would join his mother and Harold for summers in Arizona, working at whatever jobs he could find.

Harold and Hannah stayed in Tucson for two long years, returning home to California for occasional visits, and finally decided to return to Whittier permanently, because Harold was homesick and because the family's finances, severely strained by the expenses of having two separate households, were nearly exhausted.

But there was another reason for their return, a happier one. Hannah was going to have another baby. They could not risk exposing a newborn baby to life among the tuberculosis patients, so Hannah returned home and gave birth to Edward in May of 1930 in Whittier Hospital.

After Edward's birth, Harold would stay at home for brief periods, then return to Prescott when he got worse. Sometimes the family paid a woman to provide nursing care for him. Other times Hannah traveled to Prescott to nurse him herself.

"I don't know how she survived being torn like that," a Whittier friend observed.

Richard Nixon (number 12) with fellow football team members. Nixon was a poor football player but stayed on the team through sheer guts and determination. He usually sat on the bench and cheered his teammates on.

PHOTO COURTESY NATIONAL ARCHIVES.

4

The Emerging Leader

Richard's high school diploma bore a special gold seal of scholarship, awarded by the California Interscholastic Federation. He was second in his class. He had been recognized for his debating skill, his good grades, his participation in extracurricular activities. He had acted in school plays, slogged his way through seasons of football, and studied hard. As a result he won the Harvard Award as "best all-around student." He had hoped to attend Harvard College, but Hannah told him to forget his plans. "We needed Richard at home," she said.

Money was a problem, too. When he graduated from Whittier High School near the top of his class, his family could not afford to send him east to attend college. Besides, his grandfather, Franklin Milhous, had left money to Whittier College, a local Quaker school, for his grandchildren to attend.

So Richard accepted his disappointment and pursued his college career at Whittier as he did everything else in life, with hard work and determination. The result was that he made a startling impact on college life within the first month. He became the leader of a group of students who formed a new fraternity, the Orthagonians, which means Square Shooters, to compete with the established, wealthy Franklins. The Franklins always wore formal dress at their activities and were known for

34

their highbrow attitude. Nixon's fraternity decided to wear sporty sweaters with open collars. Nixon composed the club's song and helped write a play for the club to produce. He also served as director and played the male lead. He was elected as the first president of the Orthagonians as well as president of his freshman class and member of the Joint Council of the college.

He did well academically and he joined the debating team. Debating was the perfect activity for someone like Dick Nixon, who could apply his phenomenal memory and sharp mind to either side of a question. During his sophomore year, Nixon participated in more than fifty debates as a member of the Whittier College team. Here he learned the skills of cool analysis and calm public speaking that would serve him so well in the years ahead.

Even though he was adapting well to college life, Richard Nixon's home life was shadowed by the tragedy of Harold's continuing illness. Doctors urged Hannah and Frank to place Harold in a county tuberculosis hospital, but the Nixons, opposed to accepting what they considered charity, refused. They continued to nurse Harold at home. All their efforts, however, couldn't save the beloved, firstborn son.

"One morning, after we had returned to Whittier," Hannah said, "Harold asked Richard to drive him to town to buy me a birthday present. Harold chose an electric mixer."

Richard dropped Harold and the gift off, then headed for his college classes. But, when he reached the campus, word was waiting that he was needed at home. "When he got back to the house, we had to tell him Harold had died suddenly and unexpectedly," his mother remembered.

Richard took the news hard. "He sank into a deep, impenetrable silence," Hannah said. "From that time on, it seemed that Richard was trying to be three sons in one, striving even harder than before to make up to his father and me for our loss. With the death of Harold, his determination to make us proud of him seemed greatly intensified. Unconsciously, too, I think that Richard may have felt a kind of guilt that Harold and Arthur were dead and that he was alive."

After Harold's death, Richard worked harder than ever in college. He even tried to make the football team, with less success than in his academic efforts. "Dick had two left feet," a classmate told one of Nixon's early biographers. "He couldn't coordinate, but, boy, was he an inspiration. He was always talking it up. That's why the chief let him hang around, I guess."

Dick's favorite courses were in history. "As a young student Dick had the uncommon capacity to brush aside the facades of a subject and get to the heart of it," said Dr. Paul S. Smith, one of Nixon's professors. "He always completed on half a page what would take a normal A student two pages."

The young man was learning to relish leadership. And he didn't limit his efforts to serious subjects. One time Dick Nixon convinced the college trustees and faculty, as well as a conservative local leadership, to allow dancing on campus. Otherwise, he argued, students would go to the "dens of Los Angeles" to participate in the forbidden activity. Some of Nixon's later biographers have praised this as an example of Nixon's growing leadership ability. Others, more critical, cite it as an example of Nixon's willingness to compromise even his closely held religious values in order to win.

And then there was Nixon's great triumph as bonfire chairman. Every year the students held a traditional bonfire. For days, they would drag old signs and crates, furniture, and junk and pile it at the bonfire site. It was the custom for the chairman to throw the last item on the pile. Good chairmen always tried to find an outhouse for the top of the heap. A one-holer was an accomplishment, a two-holer a major victory. Richard Nixon made Whittier College history in 1933 when he set a record that still stands today. Somehow he produced a rare four-holer to crown the annual bonfire.

Nixon graduated in 1934, at the height of the Great Depression. There weren't many jobs available, but he had decided to attend law school. In a letter of recommendation, Whittier president Dr. Walter F. Dexter wrote, "I believe Nixon will become one of America's important, if not great leaders."

Even though Nixon's years at Whittier were filled with success and accomplishment, he still yearned to go east. He had decided that a career in law would suit his ability and his interest in government, history, and politics. He would have liked to attend Harvard, but once again, lack of money stood in his way. He did, though, receive a full-tuition scholarship to a new law school that had been endowed at Duke University in North Carolina.

After he arrived, Nixon learned that Duke had offered many such scholarships to first-year students, but would only renew them for the very best. So once again, Nixon was driven to succeed and, of course, he did. But the work was grueling and at times the young man, so far from home and friends, suffered moments of discouragement.

One night he was studying late in the library when his worries caught up with him. He was taking seven difficult courses. What would happen if he couldn't get grades good enough to keep that vital scholarship? Suddenly it seemed overwhelming. He buried his head in his hands. What was the use?

An older student walked by just then, one who had already achieved high honors. He noticed the younger man's despair. "What's wrong?" he asked.

"I'm scared. I counted thirty-two Phi Beta Kappa keys in my class," Nixon replied. "I don't believe I can stay up top in that group."

"Listen, Nixon, you needn't worry," the older student said. "You've got an iron butt."

Heartened by this encouragement, Nixon put his iron butt to good use and excelled once again, managing to juggle a killing schedule of work and study while he achieved high grades and kept his scholarship through all three difficult years.

He hoped to land a job with one of the top eastern law firms when he graduated, so he went to New York over the Christmas holidays of 1936 with two other seniors. They applied at all the prestigious firms. The other two landed good jobs. Nixon had serious talks with a big-name firm, but nothing came of it in the end. "If they had given me the job, I'm sure I would be there today, a corporation lawyer instead of vice-president," he said years later.

When he didn't get the job, Nixon looked elsewhere. One place he applied was at the FBI. But that job didn't materialize either. He later learned he had been chosen as an agent, but the position had not been funded. After graduating third in his class, he headed west once again, back home to Whittier, where he had been offered a job with a local law firm.

Whittier had grown into a large, friendly town of about twenty-five thousand people. The founding Quakers were now a minority, but the Quaker heritage was still reflected in this conservative, clean Los Angeles suburb, a place where America's emerging middle class could be comfortable.

Nixon went to work for Wingert and Beweley, Whittier's oldest law firm, and quickly earned a reputation as a hard worker. Although he bungled his first case, a real estate matter, he was soon managing a heavy load and he gradually became the firm's chief trial lawyer.

He set up a branch office in nearby La Habra and was appointed as the town attorney and police prosecutor. His highly successful technique was to outwork the opposition. He carefully researched every angle of complex cases and sometimes won simply because he was better prepared.

He also had a taste of failure when he encouraged friends and associates to invest in a business to produce frozen orange juice. The idea was a good one, as later frozen food tycoons would prove, but the company Nixon started couldn't find a way to package the frozen concentrate, and the fledgling business folded.

Nixon accepted the disappointment and continued his hard work and community involvement. He was soon president of the Whittier College Alumni Association and became a trustee of the college at age twenty-six, the youngest-ever member of that prestigious board.

He taught a college class in practical law and joined several civic and church groups. He enjoyed dramatics, so he decided to participate in the local theater group. That's how he met Pat Ryan in 1938.

Pat Ryan was a young and very pretty business teacher at Whittier High School. While working her way through the University of Southern California, she had sometimes worked as an extra in the movies, even having bit parts in two films, *Small Town Girl* and *Becky Sharp.* A friend had urged her to attend the tryouts for the local theater group's play. The same matchmaker had also talked to Dick Nixon.

"A friend told me about the beautiful new teacher who was trying out for a part at the little theater. It was suggested that I go down and take a look," he said. "I used to be something of an actor in my college days, so I did."

Dick knew Pat was the one for him from the first moment he saw her. He proposed to her that very first night. "I thought he was nuts or something," she said many years later. "I couldn't imagine that he would ever say that, because he is very much the opposite. He's more reserved."

But if it didn't seem in character to Pat, it did to Dick. He was following an old formula—set your sights high and work as hard as you can until you achieve your goals. He worked just as hard courting Pat as he had at his studies or his work.

"I admired Dick from the very beginning," Pat said. "I was having a very good time and wasn't anxious to settle down. I had all these visions of doing all sorts of things, including travel. I always wanted to travel."

After a determined two-year courtship, Dick sent Pat an engagement ring buried in a basket of flowers. She finally said yes and they were married on June 21, 1940, at the Mission Inn in Riverside. It was a small wedding with just a few members of the family present.

"The best decision I made was asking Patricia Ryan to be my wife," Nixon said shortly after his seventy-fifth birthday.

The young couple went to Mexico for their honeymoon, taking along a supply of canned food in order to save money. Their friends, however, tore all the labels off the cans, so every meal Dick and Pat ate on that trip was a surprise.

After a two-week honeymoon, they settled in Whittier and rented a small garage apartment. Pat continued to teach and Dick worked at his growing law practice. They were part of a growing circle of friends who got together at each other's houses for parties and attended the theater, opera, and movies

Richard M. Nixon, Lieutenant (jg), U.S. Navy.
PHOTO COURTESY NATIONAL ARCHIVES.

in groups. Dick was thinking about looking for a job with a large Los Angeles law firm when the war changed everyone's plans.

When the Japanese bombed Pearl Harbor, Dick sought a chance to help in the war effort and escape from the confines of life in Whittier at the same time. Because of his pacifist Quaker beliefs, he took a job in the tire-rationing section of the Office of Price Administration in Washington in January of 1942. There he learned firsthand about the problems of bureaucracy. While he was whittling away at the mass of paperwork the job involved, he began to wish for a more positive role.

His Quaker upbringing and the strong influence of his mother and grandmother made it difficult, but Dick Nixon decided to join the Navy where he was commissioned as a lieutenant junior grade. During his naval service, Nixon put his personal ambitions on hold and entered one of the most relaxed and carefree periods of his life.

Because he didn't plan a naval career there was no need to work so hard. Nixon learned to enjoy an occasional drink and indulge in the boyish camaraderie of military life. He learned to play cards and met fellow servicemen from all walks of life and all over the country. And he learned to vent some of the tension that filled his life by swearing. The profane language that shocked so many listeners to the famous Watergate tapes many years later had its roots in the South Pacific where "Nick" Nixon was stationed during the later part of the war.

Nixon was a popular officer who applied his organizational abilities to obtain hard-to-get fresh meat and liquor for his men, and he set up "Nick's Hamburger Shack," where he distributed free treats to the sailors and pilots who passed through.

During the long, boring days in the South Pacific, Nixon also learned to play poker. He brought to the game the same sharp mind, good memory, and sound strategic techniques that had characterized his educational career. The result was a nest egg of more than ten thousand dollars in poker winnings, a small fortune in those days.

5

Congressman and Senator

Before Richard Nixon could decide what to do after his discharge from the Navy, he was asked if he would be willing to run for Congress against Jerry Voorhis.

Voorhis, a Democrat, had been elected in a solid Republican district during the Great Depression and reelected four times. He was popular, especially with the press, and he seemed so solidly entrenched that a group of conservative California business leaders formed a committee to look for a Republican candidate who could beat him and win back the seat for the Republican party. Nixon was their choice, and he accepted the challenge.

In January of 1946 Nixon was released from active naval duty and came home to campaign. In the midst of all this excitement came the birth of the Nixons' first daughter, Tricia. When the baby was three weeks old, Pat Nixon left her with Hannah Nixon and went to work on her husband's campaign.

Voorhis had never faced an opponent as determined to win. Nixon, the skilled debater, challenged him to a series of five debates. The first proved a turning point.

The focus of the debate was Nixon's charge that Voorhis had been endorsed by a political action committee associated with the Communist party. Nixon made the most of the alleged link between Voorhis and the Communists because he realized that Americans were becoming increasingly uneasy with the actions of their former ally, the Soviet Union, which occupied and repressed the eastern European countries it had liberated at the end of the war. The Great Depression, which had made socialist and communist ideals appealing to some Americans, was over. Now communism was considered a serious threat, especially in the wake of Soviet aggression and expansion. Americans also worried that communism was becoming a domestic menace, especially with its growing influence in some labor unions.

Nixon's critics claim that he exaggerated the threat of communism, distorted facts, and used smear tactics in the campaign.

Defenders claim Nixon did what he had to do for the Republicans in order to win, characterizing the campaign as "politics as usual"—brutal but fair.

Nixon's hard work, debating ability, and focus on the issue of

Freshman Congressman Richard Nixon enjoys Washington's famous cherry blossoms with his wife, Pat, and his baby daughter, Tricia, in 1947.

communism resulted in an upset victory that sent him to Washington as a freshman congressman from California.

Much of the work in Congress is done by committees. In order to be effective, a new representative must learn the ins and outs of parliamentary procedure, committee operations, and the complex ways in which a bill becomes a law. Committee appointments are made by the senior member of each party, the Speaker of the House of the party who has the most members, and the Minority Leader of the other party.

Richard Nixon's potential was recognized by the new Speaker, former Minority Leader Joe Martin. Nixon would have liked a spot on the prestigious and powerful Judiciary Committee, but he wasn't too disappointed to be appointed to his second choice, the Education and Labor Committee. Another freshman was assigned to the same commmittee, the young Democrat from Massachusetts, John F. Kennedy.

New committee members drew straws to determine their seniority. Kennedy drew the shortest straw among the Democrats and Nixon drew the shortest straw among the Republicans. The result, Nixon wrote in his memoirs, was that the two of them "shared the dubious distinction of sitting at the opposite ends of the committee table, like a pair of unmatched bookends."

Congressman Nixon quickly earned a reputation for being smart, hardworking, and persuasive. Because of this he was appointed as one of nineteen members of a select committee that would travel to Europe to prepare a report on Secretary of State George Marshall's proposed plan for an economic bailout of the war-ravaged continent.

Even though a group of Nixon's early California supporters opposed the Marshall Plan and warned him against it, Nixon returned from Europe convinced that without a long-range aid program, "Europe would be plunged into anarchy, revolution, and, ultimately, communism."

Despite strong pressure from his constituents and from many Republican leaders, Nixon disregarded the risk to his career, supported the Marshall Plan, and worked hard for its passage.

Most newcomers to Congress received only one committee

assignment, but Nixon, because of his interest in fighting communist subversion, was asked to serve on a second committee, the controversial House Un-American Activities Committee.

The only bill ever to carry Nixon's name came as a result of his work on the Un-American Activities Committee. It was the Mundt-Nixon bill, which would require registration of all Communist party members and identification of all materials issued by "Communist-front" organizations. The most controversial of its provisions would establish the Subversive Activities Control Board, empowered to decide which organizations were "Communist-front."

The Mundt-Nixon bill was eventually passed by the House of Representatives, but was killed in the Senate where it received some heavy criticism. Even though the bill died, Nixon's pursuit of Communists made him a popular figure.

In July 1948 his second daughter, Julie, was born. Later that summer near the end of Congressman Nixon's first term, came the case that propelled him into the national spotlight. The House Un-American Activities Committee was trying to verify the testimony of a woman who had worked in a communist spy ring during the war. It called as a witness Whittaker Chambers, a former Communist who had left the party and became an editor of *Time* magazine.

Chambers told the committee his story. He had become a Communist in 1924 but had grown disillusioned and left the party in the late 1930s. Although he now feared and hated Communists, he said, he had once been part of a group whose goal was to infiltrate the United States government. He named other members of his group, including Alger Hiss, a graduate of Harvard Law School, who had held important government posts.

Chambers did not make a good impression and nothing might have come of his testimony if Alger Hiss had not asked for the opportunity to deny what Chambers had said about him.

Nixon has described the difference between Hiss and Chambers as striking. The elegance and poise of Hiss were a sharp contrast to the rumpled, unassuming Chambers. But Richard Nixon had doubts about Hiss, who had seemed almost too

Richard Nixon and his aide Robert Stripling examine the famous "Pumpkin Papers" in the Hiss case, which first propelled the young politician into the national spotlight.
PHOTO COURTESY NATIONAL ARCHIVES.

perfect in his eloquent self-defense. The committee was ready to drop the Hiss investigations, but Nixon wasn't convinced. The inquiry should be more thorough, he said. So the hearings continued. Chambers was called back and asked in detail about his relationship with Hiss. Hiss was then called back, and his answers seemed arrogant and evasive to Nixon, who now believed that Chambers was telling the truth and Hiss was lying.

Eventually Nixon produced microfilm of papers Hiss had allegedly given to the Russians. Chambers had hidden the film in a hollowed-out pumpkin. He had held back this critical evidence both to protect himself and because it implicated him as a spy. The evidence, nicknamed the "Pumpkin Papers," clinched the case. Because the statute of limitations had run out, Alger Hiss could not be tried as a spy, but he was eventually indicted for lying to the committee, convicted of perjury, and sent to prison for almost five years. Because of Nixon's leadership in exposing Hiss, in spite of efforts by the Truman administration and its Justice Department to close the case, he was now a nationally known figure.

Nixon capitalized on his growing reputation and decided to run for the United States Senate. His rival was a liberal Democrat, also from the House of Representatives, Helen Gahagan Douglas.

The senatorial campaign of 1950 was a controversial one; one that Nixon called "rocking, socking" and his critics called just plain dirty. Mrs. Douglas, who claimed that she was unfairly smeared by Nixon because he had implied that she was soft on communism, gave him the nickname, "Tricky Dick."

The campaign was generally considered the nastiest of Nixon's career. He compared Mrs. Douglas's voting record in Congress with that of Vito Marcantonio, an advocate of socialist programs, and implied that she was tainted with communism by association. He circulated a pamphlet, printed on pink paper, that charged, among other inflamatory things, that "she has so deservedly earned the title of 'the pink lady.' "

Another campaign incident that would later draw the attention of critics and historians was Nixon's use of a front commit-

Richard Nixon campaigns for the Senate in 1950 against Helen Gahagan Douglas.
PHOTO COURTESY NATIONAL ARCHIVES.

tee, "Democrats for Nixon," which circulated literature and rumors that Nixon had the support of the Democratic party.

Because Nixon succeeded in tainting his opponent's reputation with communism, her campaign was finished when Communist China invaded Korea and a great public outcry against Communists went up.

Nixon was swept into the United States Senate by a huge margin on the anit-Communist tide. He was well on his way up the ladder of success, but he had made some enemies along the way.

Eleanor Roosevelt, the former first lady, was one. "I have no respect for the way in which he accused Helen Gahagan Douglas of being a Communist because he knew that was how he would be elected," she said in a television interview. "He knew that she might be a liberal, but he knew quite well, having known her and worked with her, that she was not a Communist. I have always felt that anyone who wanted an election so much that they would use those means, did not have the character that I really admire in public life."

6

Vice-President

Senator Nixon's family life was private and quiet, his public life characterized by determination, intelligence, hard work, and pugnacity.

The elections of 1950 had given a much-needed boost to the Republican party, which had gained five seats in the Senate and twenty-eight in the House. Richard Nixon was one of the bright young lights of the rejuvenated party. The new California senator traveled around the country giving speeches. He criticized the Truman administration and proposed bold Republican programs. And he attracted the eyes of some powerful party leaders.

"The American people have had enough of the whining, whimpering, groveling attitude of our diplomatic representatives who talk of America's weaknesses and America's fears, rather than of America's strength and of America's courage," he said in one typical speech.

Senator Nixon was proving to be tough, informed, and increasingly popular as a speaker where he spared no mercy for the triple evils of "communism, cowardice, and corruption." Soon the party leaders were considering him for bigger things. When the popular World War II general and leader of the Allied

Senator Nixon meets with Congressman Gerald R. Ford in 1950.
PHOTO COURTESY GERALD R. FORD LIBRARY.

forces, Dwight D. Eisenhower, was nominated by the Republicans to run for president in 1952, Nixon was picked as his running mate.

"Nixon seemed an almost ideal candidate," said one Republican. "He was young, geographically right, had experience both in the House and the Senate with a good voting record, and was an excellent speaker."

One person who considered Nixon a good choice was Democratic Congressman John F. Kennedy. "I was tremendously pleased that the convention selected you for VP," Kennedy wrote Nixon. "I was always convinced that you would move ahead to the top, but I never thought it would come this quickly. You were an ideal selection and will bring to the ticket a great deal of strength."

Richard Nixon, who had been in politics only six years, was on his way to the biggest job of his career. But he hadn't come as far as he had without making political enemies. And those enemies were looking for any flaws in his seemingly impenetrable armor.

A group of his supporters in California had established a fund to pay the extra expenses of Nixon's speech-making trips. They wanted to make it easier for Nixon to continue speaking out on Republican issues without having to cover the travel costs from his modest senate salary and expense allowance.

When he became the vice-presidential nominee, word of the fund was leaked by some of Nixon's enemies within the California Republican party. The press began to ask questions.

SECRET NIXON FUND! RICH MEN'S TRUST FUND KEEPS NIXON IN STYLE FAR BEYOND HIS SALARY! screamed headlines in the *New York Post.*

Foes of Nixon stirred up the growing controversy as best they could, picketing and heckling at campaign appearances and calling on Eisenhower to remove him from the ticket.

The Republicans had been campaigning on a theme of cleaning up the corruption in Washington. Party leaders were alarmed that this issue would be taken from them if Nixon stayed on the ticket. Even Nixon's supporters were starting to waver. Eisenhower was under increasing pressure to dump him.

Nixon was devastated and torn. He didn't believe he had done anything wrong and felt that the fund could be satisfactorily explained. But he realized he had become a liability for Eisenhower. He considered withdrawing.

A change in candidates, however, would be deadly. If he left the ticket, Eisenhower's chances would also be jeopardized. Nixon needed a way to tell his story directly to the voters, so he turned to television.

The Republican party bought television time on Tuesday, September 23, 1952, right after the immensely popular Milton Berle show. Nixon, under increasing fire, took his case to the

Richard Nixon pleads for the support of the public in his famous "Checkers Speech," on September 23, 1952. The speech, which saved his place as a candidate for vice-president, drew both praise and criticism.
PHOTO COURTESY *COURIER-EXPRESS* COLLECTION, E.H. BUTLER LIBRARY, STATE UNIVERSITY COLLEGE AT BUFFALO AND BUFFALO AND ERIE COUNTY HISTORICAL SOCIETY.

public, although before the broadcast even his key supporters urged him to step aside.

As he entered the studio, a tense Nixon suppressed his fear and faced his audience. "My fellow Americans, I come before you tonight . . . as a man whose honesty and integrity has been questioned," he began. He explained the fund and how it had been used, and defended it on the basis that "Not one cent of the eighteen thousand dollars or any other money of that type ever went to me for my personal use. Every penny of it was used to pay for political expenses that I did not think should be charged to the taxpayers of the United States."

Nixon went on to provide a detailed listing of his finances. "Well, that's about it," he continued. "That's what we have and that's what we owe. It isn't very much, but Pat and I have the satifaction that every dime we've got is honestly ours. I should say this, that Pat doesn't have a mink coat. But she does have a respectable Republican cloth coat. And I always tell her that she'd look good in anything."

Then the young vice-presidential candidate delivered the line that would make the speech famous. He described a gift that had been sent from a supporter in Texas who had heard Pat say on the radio that her two children would like a puppy.

"It was a little cocker spaniel dog in a crate that he sent all the way from Texas. Black and white spotted. And our little girl, Tricia, the six-year-old, named it Checkers. And you know the kids love that dog and I just want to say this right now, that regardless of what they say about it we are going to keep it."

Nixon told the audience that he wasn't a quitter and concluded, "the decision, my friends, is not mine. I would do nothing that would harm the possibilities of Dwight Eisenhower to become president of the United States. And for that reason I am submitting to the Republican National Committee tonight, through this television broadcast, the decision that is theirs to make. Let them decide whether my position on the ticket will help or hurt. I am going to ask you to help them decide. Wire and write the Republican National Committee whether you think I should stay or whether I should get off. And whatever their decision is, I will abide by it."

Nixon was winding up his famous "Checkers Speech" when he ran out of time and the broadcast was cut off. At first he was afraid he had failed. "I loused it up, and I'm sorry," he said as he gathered up all his notes and threw them to the floor in a moment of frustration.

"You did a terrific job," his campaign manager told him.

"No, it was a flop. I couldn't get off in time," the discouraged Nixon replied.

But, far from being a flop, the speech was one of Nixon's great successes. All across the country telephone lines were busy and telegraph wires hummed with messages from the people.

"Keep Nixon," some urged.

"We like Dick," said others.

Hundreds of thousands of letters, cards, telegrams, and peti-

Richard Nixon, his wife, Pat, and daughters, Julie and Tricia, meet General Dwight D. Eisenhower and his wife, Mamie, at Washington's National Airport during the presidential campaign of 1952. Eisenhower was the Republican nominee for president and Nixon was his vice-presidential running mate.

NATIONAL PARK SERVICES ABBIE ROWE PHOTO COURTESY HARRY S. TRUMAN LIBRARY.

tions deluged Republican leaders, most of them urging that Nixon be kept on the ticket. "Senator Nixon talked his way into the hearts of millions," said a Denver newspaper.

There were, of course, critics of the speech, harsh ones. "This mawkish ooze ill became a man who might become the president of the United States," said a newspaper in Alabama. A show business newspaper called the telecast "a slick production" and columnist Walter Lippman called it "with all the magnification of modern electronics, simply mob law."

Richard Nixon became a household name because of the "Checkers Speech," but some of his enemies in later years would trace the roots of their antagonism to the same television appeal.

"It was the first of a long series of Nixon speeches that defy parody," wrote critic Frank Mankiewicz. Nixon had claimed the fund was used to save taxpayers' money, but "obviously he wasn't saving anyone a nickel, except himself. He had already used, and continued to use, every dollar of tax money he was authorized to use, and the extra funds simply replaced money he would have to spend himself."

"Not one cent of that money went for my personal use," Nixon had said in his speech.

"In fact, every penny had gone to his personal use," Mankiewicz said. "By the time this could be figured out, the pea was under another shell."

The Checkers Speech saved Nixon's vice-presidential candidacy and had made him an enormously popular public figure. But it also reinforced the feelings of those who called Richard Nixon "Tricky Dick."

Those feelings were aggravated by Nixon's tough campaign rhetoric. He denounced President Harry S. Truman and the Democratic presidential nominee, Adlai Stevenson, as "traitors to the high principles in which many of the nation's Democrats believe." Truman, he charged, was guilty of "covering up for political reasons an internal communist conspiracy in the United States."

Truman, years later, would call Richard Nixon "a shifty-eyed, goddam liar," who "not only doesn't give a damn about the

Richard Nixon worked hard during the 1952 campaign, delivering speech after speech.
WEIRTON STEEL CORPORATION PHOTO COURTESY DWIGHT D. EISENHOWER LIBRARY.

people; he doesn't know the difference between telling the truth and lying."

The Republican theme was expressed in the formula K_1C_2, which stood for the three major Republican campaign issues: the Korean War, corruption, and communism.

Republicans believed that the two-year-old war in Korea had ground to a stalemate that the military strategy of President Truman was perpetuating. Eisenhower promised that if he was elected he would go to Korea to find a way to end the war honorably.

The Republicans also felt the Truman administration had overlooked the blatant graft, bribery, and influence-peddling that they charged were rampant in Washington. The Truman administration was also, according to the Republicans, soft on communism.

"If the dry rot of corruption and communism, which has eaten deep into our body politic during the past seven years, can only be chopped out with a hatchet, then let's call for a hatchet," Nixon said.

He labeled the Democratic presidential candidate as "Adlai the Appeaser." Stevenson, Nixon said, had a degree from the "College of Cowardly Communist Containment."

"Nixonland is a land of slander and scare," charged Stevenson, "the land of push and grab and anything to win."

The United States was ready for a change in 1952. After years of depression, war, and successive Democratic administrations, the popular "Ike" was easily elected, Nixon along with him.

Nixon was shut out of Eisenhower's inner circle, however, and given almost no role in shaping policy, making decisions, or planning proposed legislation. Eisenhower's top aides were uncomfortable with the abrasive young politician. Eisenhower capitalized on Nixon's popularity and speaking ability, though, and sent him out on the road to drum up popular support for administration programs. Nixon traveled extensively, covering millions of miles on missions of international diplomacy. In 1953 he and Pat traveled for more than two months to Asia and the Far East.

This historic photo, taken at the January 20, 1953, inauguration of
Dwight D. Eisenhower, shows four presidents, left to right, Harry S.
Truman, Dwight D. Eisenhower, Richard M. Nixon, and Herbert Hoover.
PHOTO COURTESY HARRY S. TRUMAN LIBRARY.

The new vice-president and his wife are greeted by President Eisen-hower at an inaugural reception on January 20, 1953.
NATIONAL PARK SERVICES ABBIE ROWE PHOTO COURTESY HARRY S. TRUMAN LIBRARY.

During his Asian trip he met the government leaders. But, more important, he met many of the young leaders whose power and influence would grow over the next two decades, as did his own. In later years, each time he returned to Asia, he had the benefit of having met many of the most powerful leaders early in their careers.

At home, Nixon was used as Eisenhower's "hatchet man" to deal with the political issues that Ike preferred to stay above. Nixon spoke out against the once popular, but now controver-sial Senator Joseph McCarthy, whose crusade against commu-nism had benefited the Republicans at first but was now proving an embarrassment.

He traveled around the country helping Republican candi-dates in the 1954 elections. The president had decided not to campaign, so Nixon became the party's chief campaigner.

Because of his role, Nixon became the main target of the Democrats. It was discouraging, and he seriously considered

The vice-president with Mrs. Nixon.

Vice-president Nixon relaxes with his wife and their daughters, Tricia and Julie, and their dog, Checkers, at a New Jersey beach on August 16, 1953.
PHOTO COURTESY NATIONAL ARCHIVES.

getting out of the rat race and taking one of the many private sector job offers he had received. At one low point he told his campaign manager, "after this I am through with politics."

In September of 1955 the president had a heart attack. Nixon's responsibilities multiplied, and the picture changed for him. He faced the delicate job of keeping the president's powers intact, keeping the political situation under control, and running the country without upsetting any national or international applecarts.

During the six-week recovery period, Nixon walked a tightrope, criticized by some for not exercising enough leadership and castigated by others for seeking power and publicity. But he managed well and earned Eisenhower's esteem for his diplomatic management of the leadership crisis. When Eisenhower returned to Washington, thousands lined the streets to cheer.

In spite of the heart attack, Ike decided to run for a second term of office in 1956. Some of Eisenhower's advisers and other Republicans, still not comfortable with the vice-president's tough views on communism and other issues, started a "Dump Nixon" movement and urged the president to choose a different running mate. Eisenhower wavered and Nixon agonized. But Ike had been pleased with the way Nixon had performed after the heart attack, and he was growing fond of the intense young man. He finally decided to keep Nixon on the ticket, in spite of the pressure from Nixon's political antagonists. The team of Ike and Dick went on to win big in November.

The vice-president confers with President Dwight D. Eisenhower on August 21, 1954.
NATIONAL PARK SERVICE PHOTO COURTESY DWIGHT D. EISENHOWER LIBRARY.

Vice-President Nixon meets in his office with Congressman Gerald R. Ford in 1957.
PHOTO COURTESY GERALD R. FORD LIBRARY.

A year later, in November of 1957, Eisenhower suffered a stroke. It was a mild one, but it left him with a slight speech problem, an occasional difficulty in finding the right word. He made a magnificent recovery, but found his situation depressing and frustrating. Some voices were calling for him to step aside because of his health.

Nixon visited him often and was sometimes able to cheer him up. Ignore the press, Nixon advised, telling Ike that there was nothing wrong with his brain. "The trouble with most politicians is that their mouths move faster than their brains. With you it is the other way around," Nixon said.

Nixon's quip broke the tension. Ike laughed heartily for the first time in weeks.

The vice-president celebrates his forty-fourth birthday on January 9, 1957, with members of the Chowder and Marching Club, an organization of young Republican congressmen that Nixon helped organize during his freshman year in Congress. Club members banded together to increase their influence during their early years in office.
PHOTO COURTESY GERALD R. FORD LIBRARY.

President Dwight D. Eisenhower and Vice-President Richard M. Nixon
sit with Eisenhower's grandson, David, and Nixon's daughter Julie, at
the second Eisenhower inauguration on January 20, 1957. David and
Julie would meet again many years later, begin dating in college, fall
in love, and get married.
PHOTO COURTESY NATIONAL ARCHIVES.

Nixon's vice-presidency developed a pattern of performing
political chores at home and making diplomatic trips abroad to
help counteract the spread of communism in many of the
young Third World nations in Africa, Asia, and the Middle East.

In 1958, at the request of the State Department, he visited
several countries in South America where there was concern
about the growth of communism. The Central Intelligence
Agency had warned Nixon that the Communists might incite
demonstrations and commit acts of violence. The CIA had also
heard rumors of a plot to assassinate him. As it turned out,
Dick and Pat Nixon faced grave danger, especially in Caracas,
Venezuela, the last visit on the trip.

At the airport, Nixon stepped off the plane and walked toward
the waiting limousines. But a mob had arrived ahead of them.
Before the vice-president and his wife reached the shelter of an
awning, the band started to play the Venezuelan national an-
them. Nixon stopped to stand at attention.

"For a second it seemed as if it had begun to rain," Nixon remembers. "Then I realized that the crowd on the observation deck just above our heads was showering us with spit."

The Nixons and their escorts made their way to the motorcade and climbed into the safety of the cars. On the way to a central square in Caracas the motorcade was blocked by a string of vehicles parked across the street. When it stopped, swarms of violent demonstrators erupted from nearby streets.

"Here they come," said a man in the car.

Demonstrators swarmed around the vice-president's car. The mob pelted it with rocks, smashed it with pipes, and started to rock it back and forth. Nixon and the others trapped inside were in danger of their lives.

Nixon turned around to see if his wife, in the car behind them, was okay and saw, to his relief, that the mob was concentrating on his car. As the car was jolted back and forth, a Secret Service agent pulled out his gun, but Nixon told him to hold his fire, afraid that if a gun went off, the crowd would go berserk.

They were trapped for twelve long minutes, helpless victims of the unruly mob. The big car rocked higher and higher. Soon it would turn over and maybe burst into flames.

Vice-President Nixon and Senator John F. Kennedy meet with boxer Rocky Marciano in the U.S. Capitol in 1958.
PHOTO COURTESY JOHN F. KENNEDY LIBRARY.

Then the press truck ahead managed to break loose. It pulled out and blocked the way for Nixon's car, clearing a path. Once free, they stopped to make sure everyone was all right. Then Nixon decided to go to the American Embassy, where he stayed until he could leave the next day.

At home, Nixon was given a hero's welcome, drawing cheering crowds wherever he went. Although the positive response was gratifying, he never forgot how lucky they had been to get out alive.

A group of high school seniors from Sparta, Michigan, present Vice-President Nixon with a basket of apples on the steps of the Capitol, June 11, 1960. With them is their congressman, Gerald R. Ford.
PHOTO COURTESY GERALD R. FORD LIBRARY.

Senator John F. Kennedy speaks at unveiling ceremonies honoring history's most prominent senators in March 1959. On Kennedy's left are Senators Lyndon B. Johnson and Everett Dirkson. Sitting at the far left is Vice-President Richard Nixon, a former senator.
PHOTO COURTESY JOHN F. KENNEDY LIBRARY.

In 1959 Nixon went to the Soviet Union and became the highest ranking United States official to visit Nikita Khrushchev, "a crude bear of a man who had risen from the ranks," the leader of the Soviet Communist party.

"Khrushchev's rough manners, bad grammar, and heavy drinking caused many Western journalists and diplomats to underestimate him. But despite his rough edges, he had a keen mind and a ruthless grasp of power politics," Nixon wrote in his memoirs.

Nixon enjoyed sparring with Khruschev. One day the two attended a Moscow exhibition of American consumer goods. As they walked among the displays, they talked about all sorts of subjects and debated their differing systems of government.

When they reached a model American kitchen, the discussion became heated. Nixon defended the American way of life with vivid gestures, at one point poking his finger at Khrushchev's chest. A photographer captured Nixon's feisty moment and the confrontation became known as the "kitchen debate."

Because he had successfully stood up to the Russian bear, Nixon became even more popular at home.

7

The Fires of Defeat

Richard Nixon was the front-runner for the Republican nomination for president in 1960. His years of loyal service to the party and his popularity as a foe of communism insured that the Republican leadership would stay loyal to him despite the fact that New York Governor Nelson Rockefeller, also a Republican, was a contender as well.

In November of 1958, two years before the election, Nixon conferred with advisers who told him it was time to make his decision. "If you are going to be a candidate, you've got to start now," the chairman of the Republican National Committee said.

Rockefeller would present problems, the advisers thought, but Nixon could get the nomination. The real challenge was the election, where they estimated the odds at five to one against him. In spite of his slim chance, Nixon agreed to run. He had learned in the past that careful planning and hard work could overcome almost any odds.

Nixon believed, accurately as it turned out, that his most likely Democratic opponent would be Senator John F. Kennedy of Massachusetts. He also thought that Jack Kennedy would be the toughest man to beat.

Nixon knew and liked Kennedy. They had served together in the House of Representatives, and Nixon knew him to be intelligent and effective. Kennedy was also wealthy and had already

Richard Nixon, the Republican presidential nominee, campaigns in Buffalo, New York, in 1960.
BUFFALO *COURIER-EXPRESS* PHOTO BY RIC DELANEY COURTESY E.H. BUTLER LIBRARY, STATE UNIVERSITY COLLEGE AT BUFFALO AND BUFFALO AND ERIE COUNTY HISTORICAL SOCIETY.

employed a skilled staff. He had started his campaign back in 1956 and was off to a formidable head start.

Nixon decided that his best strategies were to concentrate on his duties as vice-president, to begin building a record of independence from Eisenhower, and to develop a statesmanlike image to counter the negative one that had haunted him ever since the California election which had catapulted him to power.

The presidential campaign of 1960 was one of unusual intensity for Nixon. "Jack Kennedy and I were both in the peak years of our political energy, and we were contesting great issues in a watershed period of American life and history," Nixon said in his memoirs.

The two candidates were distinctly different. "Kennedy preached the orthodox Democratic gospel of government activism," Nixon said, while he "carried the banner of constructive postwar Republicanism."

Nixon considered his strongest asset to be the fact that, since the trip to Caracas and his confrontation with Khrushchev, he was "probably the best known political figure in the country after Eisenhower."

Kennedy's most important advantages, Nixon felt, were his wealth and the appeal of his personal style. Kennedy's biggest disadvantage, according to Nixon, was his lack of experience.

It would be a tough campaign, Nixon believed. But he was looking forward to the challenge. "I knew it would be an uphill battle, but I felt I could win." It was a combination of bad luck and bad judgment that cost Nixon the closest presidential election in history.

Things had started off well. His trip to Russia and his masterful handling of Khrushchev had enhanced his reputation as a statesman and patriot. The polls showed him leading Kennedy 53 percent to 47 percent. He was able to intercede and help avoid a threatened steel strike, with a resulting increase in his popularity. He easily won the nomination and cemented the backing of the Republican party solidly behind him.

Several factors were working against him, however. A leading economist advised Nixon that the economy was slowing down and would slump in October, just before the election. Nixon urged Eisenhower and his cabinet to take steps to improve the economic outlook, but Eisenhower didn't agree with the forecast and didn't think it right to tamper with the economy for political reasons.

Then came the infamous U-2 incident. Shortly before Eisenhower and Khrushchev were due to meet at a Paris summit conference, the Soviets shot down a CIA U-2 spy plane over the USSR and captured the pilot.

Khrushchev ranted and raved and called off the summit. There was a great public outcry at home and the administration's handling of the situation drew harsh criticism. Nixon's chances of victory dimmed.

In an effort to balance the ticket with an opponent from Kennedy's home state of Massachusetts, Nixon had picked Henry Cabot Lodge as his running mate, but was disappointed when Lodge turned out to be a mild campaigner. He hoped that his own hard work would make the difference. He threw himself into an exhausting campaign, promising to visit all fifty states before the election. The pace was killing, but he continued to push.

At one campaign stop he banged his knee on a car door. It hurt, but he didn't give the incident much thought. Nor did he slow down. The injured knee continued to trouble him. He began to feel weak and sick. Medical tests showed that the knee was infected so badly that Nixon would have to be hospitalized and given massive doses of antibiotics.

He lay frustrated in a hospital bed, enduring agonizing injections, while he fell behind Kennedy and lost valuable campaign time.

When he was released, still tired and sore, he tried to make up for lost time by doubling his already savage schedule. Within three days he was running a fever of over 103 degrees, though he continued to campaign strenuously.

When the time came for his first historic television debate with Kennedy, Nixon was exhausted, sick, and underweight. Kennedy was tan and fit. The debate was a disaster. Although most observers called the discussion of the issues a draw, the audience responded to the contrasting images of the two men.

These photos of the two candidates, Democrat John F. Kennedy and Republican Richard M. Nixon, were taken during 1960 presidential campaign.
PHOTO COURTESY JOHN F. KENNEDY LIBRARY.

Nixon speaks at a rally in his honor during the 1960 campaign.
BUFFALO *COURIER-EXPRESS* PHOTO BY I.R. SORGI COURTESY E.H. BUTLER LI-
BRARY, STATE UNIVERSITY COLLEGE AT BUFFALO AND BUFFALO AND ERIE
COUNTY HISTORICAL SOCIETY.

Nixon later observed that it was a sad commentary on the
effect of television that the substance of the debates was of less
importance than the physical appearances of the two candidates.

Although he was better rested and prepared for the remaining
debates, the damage was done. The campaign lost heart and
the last-minute edge went to the vigorous Kennedy. The popular
vote was so close that only two-tenths of one percent separated
the victorious Kennedy from the vanquished Nixon.

The narrow loss was even harder to accept because there
were indications of massive voter fraud in Illinois, Texas, and
Missouri. If only a few of the crooked votes that had piled up for
Kennedy had been disallowed, the election outcome would have
been different.

There was an outcry among many of Nixon's supporters, who urged him to demand recounts in the three states. Nixon briefly considered the idea of contesting the results, but decided not to in the best interests of the nation. Times were too difficult, international relations too tense for there to be even an appearance of disunity over the American presidency. Nixon let the vote stand rather than plunge into a squabble that would threaten the stability of the presidency.

So it was that he found himself, on January 6, 1960, presiding over his own "funeral." As vice-president, he served as head of the Senate. In that capacity it was his duty to perform the ceremonial counting of the electoral college votes and announce to a joint session of Congress that John F. Kennedy had defeated Richard M. Nixon.

"I don't think we could have a more striking and eloquent example of the stability of our constitutional system and of the proud tradition of the American people of developing, respecting, and honoring institutions of self-government," Nixon said. He received a standing ovation.

Then came his last official act, the inauguration. He drove to the inauguration ceremony with Lyndon Johnson, who had been elected vice-president. When Kennedy had been sworn in and given his stirring inaugural address, Nixon was the first to shake hands with the new president. He wished him well.

Then, while the new guard in Washington paraded in victory toward the White House, the Nixons and the Eisenhowers had a farewell lunch. That night, private citizen Nixon had a quiet dinner at home with his family.

Tricia and Julie told him that if there hadn't been cheating on the voting in Chicago, they would have been eating in the White House.

"This is no time for bitterness," Richard Nixon told his daughters. "One benefit of losing the election is that I'll be home for dinner more often."

After dinner Nixon paid a quiet visit to the Capitol. He walked up the Capitol stairs. A surprised guard let him in, and he walked down the corridor to the rotunda to where the dome rises above it.

The Nixon family in 1960.
PHOTO COURTESY HARRY S. TRUMAN LIBRARY.

A balcony looks out over the Washington Monument and the distant Lincoln Memorial. He stood there for several minutes, absorbing the peace of the moment. He thought about all the great experiences since he had first come to Washington as a green freshman congressman in 1947. Then he turned to go inside.

He suddenly stopped short, struck by the thought that this was not necessarily the end. He promised himself to return some day.

Nixon still hoped that he could win the presidency, perhaps by running against Kennedy again in 1964. In the meantime, the family moved back to California and he joined a Los Angeles law firm. He wrote a book about some of his experiences, *Six Crises*. He served as the titular head of the Republican party, making frequent appearances and speeches. He sometimes criticized President Kennedy as a leader of the "loyal opposition."

Many of Nixon's friends and advisers thought he would have a better chance of getting the 1964 nomination and winning the election if he was already holding public office. They urged him to run for governor of California in 1962.

Nixon had some serious reservations, but eventually he decided to make the run. It turned out to be a mistake, although early polls showed he could beat the incumbent governor, Pat Brown.

Opposition quickly began to build. An extreme conservative ran against Nixon in the Republican primary. Many rabid right-wingers bitterly refused to support Nixon when their candidate lost.

Members of the ultra-right-wing John Birch Society had infiltrated some Republican party groups. The John Birchers hurt his candidacy in two ways: first by voting against Nixon in the primary, and second by tainting the image of the Republican party with their fanaticism, swaying moderate voters toward the Democrats.

Nixon believed that the press was unfair, too, concentrating on smears and personal attacks rather than issues. And he was

Richard Nixon, the former vice-president, plays the piano at a Chowder and Marching Club meeting honoring House of Representatives Minority Leader Gerald R. Ford on February 24, 1965. Others in the photo include, left to right, Representatives Robert Michel of Illinois, Charlotte Reid of Illinois, Les Arends of Illinois, Gerald Ford of Michigan, and Melvin Laird of Wisconsin.
PHOTO COURTESY GERALD R. FORD LIBRARY.

frequently criticized for using California's governorship as a stepping-stone back to Washington.

The campaign wasn't going well. The Republican party was divided, the press hostile, and Nixon was frequently heckled by extremists. Then came a national crisis that overshadowed local issues in the campaign and gave the Democrats a huge push.

In late October, just two weeks before the election, President Kennedy told Americans in a dramatic television speech that the Russians had moved nuclear missiles into Cuba, just ninety miles off the coast of Florida. He announced a naval blockade off Cuba and demanded that Khrushchev order the missiles dismantled and returned to the Soviet Union.

The Cuban Missile Crisis kept the world on the brink of nuclear war for two full days before Khrushchev finally backed down. It dominated the news during the final days of the 1962 campaign. Nixon gave public support to Kennedy's actions, rallying behind the president during an international crisis.

But the crisis and Kennedy's success hurt Nixon's candidacy. Nixon knew any chance he had of narrowing Brown's lead in the polls was now gone, but, he said, "We had to play the dreary drama through to its conclusion on election night."

And dreary it was. Nixon went to bed at three o'clock in the morning. The vote was still close, but he knew the state well and predicted that the votes in the precincts not yet reported would not be enough to save the day.

When he awoke a few short hours later to learn he had lost, he sent his press secretary to read a concession statement. But reporters wanted Nixon in person. They badgered the press secretary. At first Nixon refused, but the television in his hotel room showed the angry reporters demanding him and Nixon, also angry, decided to go to the press conference.

His pent-up frustration resulted in a well-known moment when he blasted back at the press. He told the reporters that in his long career, he had never before complained about their reporting to their editors and publishers and had endured their criticisms without rancor.

For sixteen years, Nixon charged, ever since the Hiss case, reporters had used every opportunity to attack him. "Just think how much you're going to be missing," he said. "You won't have Nixon to kick around anymore, because, gentlemen, this is my last press conference."

8

The Great Comeback

The November 16, 1962, issue of *Time* magazine pronounced the political demise of Richard Nixon. "Barring a miracle, his political career ended last week," it said. And ABC television broadcast "The Political Obituary of Richard Nixon" in which a panel of analysts said Nixon was hopelessly washed up.

Tired and discouraged, Nixon decided to make some changes in his life. Influential business friends secured him a job with a major New York law firm and the family bought a Fifth Avenue apartment. Nixon kept a long-standing promise to his wife and daughters and took them on a trip to Europe. They traveled with old friends and enjoyed every moment together.

While the Nixon family was in Rome, President Kennedy was also there on a state visit. One afternoon the phone rang in their hotel room. It was Jack Kennedy, who said that he had heard the Nixons were in Rome and just wanted to say hello. It was the last time Nixon talked to him.

The move to New York, Nixon believed, had cemented the end of one career and marked the start of another. He had no political base in the home state of his old rival, Nelson Rockefeller. He would, for the first time in his adult life, be out of the political mainstream.

He settled into a pleasant routine of building the business of his law firm, writing, seeing old friends, and making new ones. He felt he had made the right choice. Occasionally he was urged to run for office again, but he wasn't tempted.

At this time the Republican party was being divided by conservative and liberal factions; the conservatives led by Barry Goldwater of Arizona, the liberals by Nelson Rockefeller. Nixon supporters urged him to step in to avoid a major split in the party. Nixon shared their concerns, but his instinct was not to get involved, since he considered Kennedy unbeatable.

A series of fateful events, however, changed the entire American political scene. Nixon flew to Dallas, Texas, on November 20, 1963, to attend a business meeting. He returned home on November 22. On his way to the airport he noticed flags along the motorcade route to be followed later that day by President Kennedy.

When he arrived in New York, he took a cab from the airport. The cab was stopped at a red light when a frantic man ran up. "Do you have a radio in your cab? I just heard that Kennedy was shot."

When the cab pulled up in front of Nixon's building, the doorman was crying. "Oh, Mr. Nixon, have you heard, sir? They've killed President Kennedy."

The assassination stunned the nation, plunging the American people into a period of shocked mourning. Although Nixon had been critical of Kennedy's performance as president, he admired Kennedy's competitive spirit and could imagine how terrible the Kennedy family must feel. "I remembered how I had felt when first Arthur and then Harold had died, and I wished there was something that I could do to ease the Kennedys' grief," Nixon said in his memoirs.

Kennedy's death marked a fundamental change in American society, ending an upbeat, energetic era and ushering in a time of tumult, dissent, and social violence.

On the political scene, Barry Goldwater's strength in the Republican party began to build, and President Lyndon Johnson was able to successfully pick up the fallen reins of leadership. According to Nixon, Johnson's first months in the White House were marked by "consummate skill."

The Kennedy assassination also marked a change in Richard Nixon's thinking about his own career. Nixon had planned to write a book about the coming presidential election, but he shelved those plans in favor of a more active role in Republican politics. The possibility of another try at the presidency was no longer remote.

Nixon found life outside the political mainstream dull, and he sought both escape and a return to the perks of power politics in foreign travel. In his own country he was one of many defeated candidates. Overseas he was received by heads of state, his opinions sought and respected, the hospitality as sumptuous as when he had been vice-president. He visited Lebanon, Pakistan, Malaysia, Thailand, Vietnam, the Philippines, Hong Kong, Taiwan, and Japan.

Nixon thought that Johnson would be as unbeatable as Kennedy in the 1964 election. The Republican battle for the nomination was likely to be bruising and one he would be better off to stay well above. Instead, he could cultivate party leaders and insure their loyalty by continuing his speaking, fund-raising, and campaigning on behalf of various Republican candidates for state, local, and national offices. He continued to travel extensively and polish his image as a statesman and foreign policy expert.

The archconservative Barry Goldwater received the Republican nomination in 1964, creating bitter fissures in the party structure. Nixon knew that the result was likely to be a Democratic landslide that would sweep Lyndon Johnson into a term of his own and carry hundreds of Democrats on his coattails.

Nixon introduced Goldwater's acceptance speech at the convention with a masterful appeal for party unity, one that earned the nominee a rousing ovation as he entered the convention hall. To his dismay, however, Goldwater delivered a strident, divisive speech, which included two statements that would haunt Goldwater and all Republicans for a long time to come—"Extremism in the defense of liberty is no vice!" Goldwater had ranted. "Moderation in the pursuit of justice is no virtue."

Goldwater not only failed to heal the party wounds, Nixon felt, he had "opened new wounds and rubbed salt in them."

In spite of the disastrous effect of the Goldwater nomination on the Republican party in 1964, however, and the resulting Johnson landslide, Nixon ended up in a strong position for 1968. He campaigned for Goldwater, always careful to dissociate himself from the candidate's extremist positions while he pleaded for party unity. He earned the gratitude of many Republican candidates and leaders, all of whom would be happy to repay Nixon with their support in 1968. He emerged as an elder statesman of the Republican party.

After Goldwater's defeat, Nixon was free to continue his travels, plan strategy for the next presidential election, and serve as the most visible Republican critic of the Johnson administration. He already knew from his visits to Asia that Johnson was in trouble in Vietnam. He knew, too, that there was no easy way out and that the bitter Vietnam war was likely to cost Johnson his popularity. Lyndon Johnson would be beatable in 1968, Nixon believed; and he intended to be the one to beat him.

Goldwater had almost destroyed the party in 1964. Republicans lost thirty-seven seats in the House of Representatives, two in the Senate, and over five hundred in state legislatures. But no one blamed Nixon for the fiasco. In fact, if it hadn't been for Nixon, many felt, the debacle would have been even worse.

In 1965 Nixon authorized some of his old friends to begin raising money to finance his travels on behalf of the party, and also to give him a head start on the long road to the presidency.

He was in an ideal position. He could maintain a high profile among Republicans, keeping the leadership indebted to him and giving him a strong political base. He could attack Johnson and the Democrats from the sidelines, earning headlines for himself and, at the same time, build an effective campaign organization ready to move into high gear at the right time.

He started by holding a press conference that was calculated to solidify his position and dispose of the major threat within his own party, Nelson Rockefeller. Those who had divided the party in the past could not expect to unite it in the future, he said of Rockefeller. He called Rockefeller a spoilsport who should no longer be regarded as a national party leader.

Nixon then waited for the Democrats to make mistakes. There were messy times ahead. The great civil rights movement was creating a backlash. Expensive "Great Society" programs were criticized by many business leaders as a threat to the economy. The war in Vietnam was unpopular, deadly, and increasingly divisive. America was entering a period of tumult.

Nixon enjoyed the 1966 campaign. He gave his enthusiastic support to Republican candidates, raised money, made speeches, traveled tirelessly, and earned the gratitude of thousands of Republicans. His efforts paid off. The Republicans won back 47 House seats, 3 Senate seats, 8 governorships, and 540 seats in state legislatures.

Nixon was now poised for a remarkable comeback. He began his formal campaign for the presidency at a press conference on February 2, 1968, in Manchester, New Hampshire.

"Gentlemen," he announced, "this is *not* my last press conference." He told the reporters that he was entering the New Hampshire primary and would seek the Republican nomination. Nixon won 78 percent of the vote in the uncontested New Hampshire primary and went on to win significant primary victories in other states. His success was so positive that just before the takeoff of his chartered flight from Madison, Wisconsin, the flight attendant announced, "On behalf of your crew and North Central Airlines, I would like to welcome you to the next portion of your flight to the White House."

Although Nixon fought off some ineffective opposition for the nomination, the Democrats were embroiled in a desperate scramble for the top spot on their ticket. Lyndon Johnson's popularity had plummeted. His Vietnam policy was opposed by harsh critics on both sides and his social programs were mired in controversy. Everywhere Johnson went, he sparked loud demonstrations. "Hey, hey, LBJ. How many kids did you kill today?" chanted antiwar activists while dissidents within his own party plotted to dump him.

Johnson stunned the world with a surprise announcement at the end of a speech on Vietnam. On March 31, he told the

Richard Nixon, once again a Republican presidential nominee, confers with President Lyndon B. Johnson at the LBJ Ranch in Texas, on August 10, 1968.
PHOTO COURTESY LYNDON B. JOHNSON LIBRARY.

American people that he couldn't devote any time to party politics when so much was at stake in Vietnam, and that his job as president required all of his energy and ability. "Accordingly, I shall not seek, and I will not accept, the nomination of my party for another term as your president."

Johnson's announcement heated up the scramble for the Democratic nomination. Robert Kennedy, the late president's younger brother, entered the race. He was the likeliest nominee, in Nixon's opinion. The Democratic infighting grew bitter, the distant war raged, and the streets at home were scenes of more and more demonstrations.

Then came a series of tragedies. On April 4, Martin Luther King, Jr., the popular civil rights leader, was assassinated in Tennessee, touching off a series of riots and racial violence throughout the country.

Bobby Kennedy was shot in June just after winning the California Democratic primary. He died the next day, leaving a leadership vacuum in his party.

On the comeback trail. Richard Nixon campaigns in Buffalo, New York, in October 1968.
BUFFALO *COURIER-EXPRESS* PHOTO COURTESY E.H. BUTLER LIBRARY, STATE UNIVERSITY COLLEGE AT BUFFALO AND BUFFALO AND ERIE COUNTY HISTORICAL SOCIETY.

In the southern United States a former governor of Alabama, George Wallace, was trying to win the presidency through a third party candidacy. His platform of white supremacy was repugnant to many Americans, but it threatened to draw vital support from both Democrats and Republicans. Although he had no hope of winning the presidency, Wallace loomed as a threat that could deprive both majority party candidates of a clear victory in the electoral college, thus throwing the election into the House of Representatives and perhaps precipitating a constitutional crisis.

Nixon won his party's nomination at the Republican National Convention in Miami Beach, Florida, easily deflecting challenges from conservative Ronald Reagan and liberal Nelson Rockefeller. In order to help generate support in the south, Nixon picked Spiro Agnew, the governor of Maryland, to be his running mate.

"Agnew's one of the most underrated men in America, a man who can show poise under pressure," Nixon told the press. "You can look him in the eye, and you know he's got it. He has

a good heart. He's an old-fashioned patriot, highly controlled."
He paused, then added in an ironic, if unintended, prophecy: "If
the guy's got it, he'll make it. If not, I've made a bad choice."

The Democrats nominated Johnson's vice-president, Hubert
Humphrey, at a strife-torn convention in Chicago, marred by
vicious infighting on the convention floor and violence outside
in the streets, where young demonstrators battled with police.
Humphrey selected Senator Edmund Muskie of Maine as his
running mate and began his campaign as an apologist for
Johnson's Vietnam policy, leading a badly divided party.

Nixon ran a relaxed, confident campaign, one designed to
enhance voter perception of the "new Nixon." He had a well-

Nixon campaigns in Buffalo, New York, in October 1968.
BUFFALO *COURIER-EXPRESS* PHOTO BY RIC DELANEY COURTESY E.H. BUTLER
LIBRARY, STATE UNIVERSITY COLLEGE AT BUFFALO AND BUFFALO AND ERIE
COUNTY HISTORICAL SOCIETY.

oiled machine this time, headed by his law partner, John Mitchell.

It was a modern campaign that made extensive use of computers, direct mail, television, and pacing. Nixon projected confidence and statesmanship, carefully avoiding the harsh rhetoric of the past. He kept his speeches bland and general, leaving a substantive discussion of the issues to a series of position papers that few actually read. It was a campaign of images.

One of his key campaigners was a Los Angeles advertising executive named Bob Haldeman. Haldeman was a new-breed politician, an image maker. He was the one who first suggested that Nixon abandon the old-fashioned, whistle-stop stumping and concentrate on the images that could make best use of television.

Haldeman argued that a candidate could make hundreds of speeches and still only manage direct contact with relatively few potential new supporters. And Nixon already knew how disastrous a frantic pace could be. His relentless efforts had sapped his energies in 1960 and had been a factor in his losing to Kennedy.

Nixon decided Haldeman was right. He needed to be well rested and relaxed to project the right image. He needed to be protected from too many demands on his time. The briskly efficient Haldeman became the watchdog who guarded Nixon's gates.

Nixon's daughter, Julie, remembers that the tone of the campaign changed as Haldeman's role grew. "The hectic, but intimate atmosphere," Julie wrote in a biography of her mother, "acquired a businesslike, no-nonsense tempo."

"What's happened? The fun's gone," said a close family friend.

But the strategy worked. Nixon beat Humphrey by half a million votes. The man who had been pronounced politically dead in 1962 was the president-elect of the United States. Richard Nixon had come back.

Outgoing President Lyndon B. Johnson and incoming President Richard M. Nixon on Inauguration Day, January 20, 1969.
PHOTO COURTESY LYNDON B. JOHNSON LIBRARY.

9

President at Last

Richard Nixon placed his hand on the two Milhous family Bibles held by his wife. They were both open to the Book of Isaiah. "They shall beat their swords into plowshares, and their spears into pruning hooks: nation shall not lift up sword against nation, neither shall they learn war any more," the passages said.

The chief justice of the Supreme Court administered the oath of office on January 20, 1969. Then the new president of the United States, Richard Milhous Nixon, stood in the cold drizzle and talked about the need for peace. The single biggest problem facing him was the war in faraway Vietnam. It was a complex, bitter, and divisive war, one that had been a mistake to get into and one that was proving difficult to get out of.

"The greatest honor history can bestow is the title of peacemaker. This honor now beckons America," Nixon said in his inaugural address. "If we succeed, generations to come will say of us now living that we mastered our moment, that we helped make the world safe for mankind. This is our summons to greatness."

Richard Nixon takes the oath of office as the thirty-seventh president of the United States on January 20, 1969.
PHOTO COURTESY NATIONAL ARCHIVES.

After his speech and a luncheon in the Capitol came the traditional inaugural parade to the White House. Nixon had invited the high school band from Whittier, California, his hometown, to march. It was planned to be a festive, triumphant occasion. But the parade route was lined with angry demonstrators, intent on expressing their dissatisfaction with the war in Vietnam. They hurled sticks, stones, and beer cans at the president's car.

"Those first hours of the presidency were a sobering reminder of the deep discontent in the country and of the urgent need for action," wrote Nixon's daughter, Julie.

After a whirlwind day that included receptions, parties, and several inaugural balls, the Nixon family returned to the White House at two o'clock in the morning, tired but happy. A new family member was with them, Julie's new husband, David Eisenhower, the grandson of President Eisenhower.

After exploring the White House residential quarters, the new president sat down at a piano and played "Rustle of Spring," a

President Nixon plays the piano for former President Harry S. Truman while Pat Nixon and Bess Truman look on, March 21, 1969.
PHOTO COURTESY HARRY S. TRUMAN LIBRARY.

piece he had been taught years ago by his Aunt Jane. Then he played a special song he had composed for Pat before they were married while everyone relaxed, pausing to enjoy the special moment.

"It's good to be home," Pat said quietly.

Nixon remembers that everyone looked up. The White House was now their home.

Nixon had once described himself as an introvert in an extrovert's profession. He had always been a man who needed solitude, who needed to retreat into his own world and reflect on what course of action was best. "The decisions that are important are the decisions that must be made alone," he has said.

Because of his need to be alone, he frequently isolated himself in his office. He limited contact with others in government, usually preferring to communicate in writing. He appointed Bob Haldeman as a chief of staff who served as a buffer between the Oval Office and the rest of the world.

This management style was perceived as aloof and arrogant by some in government and by members of the press. Nixon had never been comfortable with the press, and the relationship grew more and more strained. Haldeman, National Security Adviser Henry Kissinger, and another assistant, John Ehrlichman, were nicknamed "The Berlin Wall" for their role in isolating the president, not only from the press and the public, but from some of his own cabinet members and Republican party leaders as well.

The major issue facing the new president was the war in Vietnam. In spite of growing antiwar protests, Nixon believed that the United States should not abandon the effort to save South Vietnam from communism. He hoped that a negotiated peace would be possible if the North Vietnamese could be convinced that a military victory for them was impossible.

Nixon's plans for Vietnam included secret negotiations by his expert on foreign policy and national security, Henry Kissinger; stepped-up bombing and military actions to root out communist sanctuaries and supply lines; and strengthening the South Vietnamese army with supplies, training, and other assistance. He wanted to prepare the South Vietnamese to take over the fight.

Early in the new administration the North Vietnamese tested the new president by launching a small but savage offensive into South Vietnam. Nixon believed it was a deliberate test. He responded by increasing the military action to let the Communists know he was serious and to induce them to negotiate. On March 17, 1969, B-52 bombers peppered the communist sanctuaries inside the Cambodian border, but the operation was kept secret. Nixon told only two senators from the Senate Armed Services Committee and the necessary military authorities.

He felt that the North Vietnamese wouldn't be able to protest the secret bombing because they officially denied having any troops in Cambodia.

Another reason for keeping the bombing secret was the threat of massive demonstrations at home. Because his administration was so new, Nixon wanted to "provoke as little public

President Nixon seems relaxed and happy as he arrives in Independence, Missouri, for a visit with former President Harry S. Truman.
PHOTO COURTESY HARRY S. TRUMAN LIBRARY.

outcry as possible." He was pleased with the effect of the secret bombings and the steady decline in American casualties.

Nixon's first trip as president was a highly successful one to Europe, where he met with heads of state and leaders of several countries. He wanted to consult with allies before negotiating with potential adversaries and to show the world that he was not completely obsessed with Vietnam. He also wanted to show Americans that their president could still command respect and enthusiasm abroad, despite antiwar demonstrations at home.

The trip renewed his confidence in his ability to handle foreign policy and offered an escape from the turmoil at home.

There were highs and lows during Nixon's first year as president. A low came on March 28, 1969, when former President Dwight David Eisenhower, who had been in failing health for a number of years, died.

A high point came that first summer when two Americans, Neil Armstrong and Buzz Aldrin, became the first humans ever to set foot on the moon. Nixon was jubilant with the success of the historic Apollo Eleven mission and flew to the South Pacific for the splashdown. He was there waiting to welcome America's newest heros back to Earth.

From the Apollo splashdown, he traveled on around the world, stopping in Guam, the Philippines, Indonesia, Thailand, South Vietnam, India, Pakistan, Romania, and Britain. The trip was given the code name Moonglow in honor of the historic event.

While Nixon was traveling, with the attention of the world focused on his visit to South Vietnam, Henry Kissinger was conducting secret negotiations with the North Vietnamese.

By fall, however, there was still no substantial progress and protests were spreading on American college campuses. In a speech on November 3, Nixon told the American people that he was going to keep the commitment of the United States to South Vietnam and continue the fighting until the Communists agreed to negotiate a fair and honorable peace or until the South Vietnamese were capable of defending themselves.

"And so tonight, to you, the great silent majority of my fellow Americans, I ask for your support," the president appealed.

Long distance! A jubilant President Nixon talks with the first men to walk on the moon on July 20, 1969, while millions of Americans watch at home.
PHOTO COURTESY NATIONAL ARCHIVES.

Nixon's Silent Majority speech was condemned by many members of the press and political opponents, but it struck a responsive chord in some segments of American society. Thousands called or wrote the White House with expressions of support while at the same time Nixon's critics claimed that he was trying to divide the country and turn Americans against each other.

Nixon felt that the response to his speech was a sign of strong support for his Vietnam policy, but critics disagreed. The number of antiwar protesters grew. Thousands of young American men continued a form of protest that had begun during the term of President Johnson by refusing to enter military service, in defiance of draft laws.

In the spring of 1970 Nixon authorized an invasion of Vietnam's neighbor, Cambodia, because of enemy sanctuaries across its borders. The move resulted in strong protests at home. In May, at Kent State University in Ohio, the National Guard was called out to put down student demonstrations. Frightened guardsmen panicked and fired into a crowd of protesters. Four students were killed.

Now thousands of antiwar activists arrived in Washington to demonstrate against the Cambodian incursion and the Kent State killings. Despite the protests, the president stuck to his program of phased withdrawal and negotiations.

During this period of bitter social upheaval, President Nixon

A pleasant moment, July 22, 1969.
PHOTO COURTESY NATIONAL ARCHIVES.

was also having problems in other areas. He wanted to make progress in domestic affairs. He wanted to appoint justices to the Supreme Court who shared his conservative views of constitutional interpretation. He wanted Congress to pass new programs that would streamline government and make it more efficient. He sought congressional cooperation to reform taxes and government spending, reorganize foreign aid programs, reform the electoral process, and, most important to him, restore "law and order" to a society plagued with poverty, crime, and violence.

Nixon quickly learned, though, that all his expertise, enthusiasm, ability, and determination could not overcome the fact that he was the first president in 120 years to begin an administration while the Senate and the House of Representatives were controlled by the opposing party. Despite his active campaigning in the congressional elections of 1970, the Republicans lost nine seats in the House of Representatives and eleven governorships. The Republican gain of two seats was not enough to offset the influence of a hostile, Democratic-controlled Congress. Of the more than forty proposals for domestic programs to Congress in Nixon's first year, only two passed.

Nixon blamed the Democratic Congress for failure to pass his programs. Some critics suggest that his politically inexperienced and sometimes arrogant White House staff was also a factor.

Nixon's concerns about the Democratic Congress were equalled by his opinion of the Supreme Court. He thought that the Supreme Court had become far too liberal in the civil liberties it extended to criminals and in its rulings on civil rights and desegregation. When Chief Justice Earl Warren retired, Nixon appointed Warren Burger, a conservative, to replace him.

The president's appointments to the Supreme Court have to be confirmed, or voted on, by the Senate before appointees can take their places on the court bench. Burger's confirmation was quickly approved. But the next time there was a Supreme Court vacancy, Nixon faced potent opposition.

Twice he named conservative judges from the South, but

President Nixon and Governor Nelson Rockefeller of New York, old Republican rivals, campaign together in New York State. Rockefeller would later be named vice-president by President Gerald Ford.
BUFFALO *COURIER-EXPRESS* PHOTO COURTESY E.H. BUTLER LIBRARY, STATE UNIVERSITY COLLEGE AT BUFFALO AND BUFFALO AND ERIE COUNTY HISTORICAL SOCIETY.

both choices were bitterly opposed in the Senate and labeled by some as mediocre, incompetent, and racist. Senate investigations said the first nominee had business interests that conflicted with his judicial duties, and that the second had run for political office many years earlier as an advocate of white supremacy. Both men were rejected, Nixon believed, because of their judicial philosophies and southern roots.

"I have reluctantly concluded that it is not possible to get confirmation for a judge on the Supreme Court of any man who believes in the strict construction of the Constitution, as I do, if he happens to come from the South," Nixon said when he announced his third appointee, Harry A. Blackmun, who was confirmed without incident.

In his early years in office Nixon took a firm stand on behalf of the beleaguered environment, pleasing even his critics. He was eventually responsible for the creation of the new and vital Environmental Protection Agency. But progress in civil rights

President Richard M. Nixon in 1970.
WHITE HOUSE PHOTO COURTESY *COURIER-EXPRESS* COLLECTION, E.H. BUTLER LIBRARY, STATE UNIVERSITY COLLEGE AT BUFFALO AND BUFFALO AND ERIE COUNTY HISTORICAL SOCIETY.

slowed, and criticism of the federal government's sluggish enforcement of civil rights laws came from all sides, even from within the administration itself.

Nixon also faced a possible economic recession with prices of consumer products and wages rising while production of goods declined and unemployment grew. He proposed a ceiling on federal spending, which the Democratic Congress refused to enact.

High interest rates and reduced government spending would slow the recession, Nixon believed. He cut funding for welfare, health, and social programs and eventually dismantled the Office of Economic Opportunity, the major weapon of former President Lyndon Johnson's Great Society and War on Poverty.

Unfortunately, slashes in spending on domestic programs to help stop inflation and balance the budget were offset by the massive increases in military spending necessitated by the war in Vietnam.

After two years Nixon admitted that, without congressional cooperation, his economic policy was not working and placed controls on wages and prices. Regrettably, the controls came too late to check the continuing inflation. Adding to economic woes was a sharp increase in the cost of energy caused by the tripling of gas and oil prices in 1973 and 1974 when the Organization of Petroleum Exporting Countries (OPEC) imposed an oil embargo. OPEC was retaliating for United States support of Israel during the brief Yom Kippur War against Syria and Egypt.

Nixon tried to lift the burden of property taxes by starting an innovative federal revenue-sharing program that returned tax dollars directly to state and local governments. But the impact of the program was blunted by additional welfare costs for state and local governments in the wake of domestic cutbacks.

The American public may have found Richard Nixon controversial in his first term as president, but it liked and admired his wife and family and followed the White House romance of Nixon's older daughter, Tricia, with avid interest. Tricia's marriage to Edward Cox in a Rose Garden ceremony at the White House was a pleasant highlight of 1971.

However, as the politically embattled president's domestic

President Nixon dances with his daughter Tricia Nixon Cox, at her
June 12, 1971, White House wedding.
PHOTO COURTESY NATIONAL ARCHIVES.

President and Mrs. Nixon visit Rochester, New York, on June 19, 1971. Pat Nixon looked "rested and glowing—amazingly so for so soon after Tricia's wedding," reported one area newspaper.
BUFFALO *COURIER-EXPRESS* PHOTO COURTESY E.H. BUTLER LIBRARY, STATE UNIVERSITY COLLEGE AT BUFFALO AND BUFFALO AND ERIE COUNTY HISTORICAL SOCIETY.

programs foundered, he suffered increasing criticism and again turned to foreign affairs to find success. A crowning achievement of the Nixon presidency came in early 1972 when Nixon reestablished relations with China and became the first president ever to visit that vital country.

He had learned over the years that foreign policy could not continue to be based on the overly simple view of the world as if it were in the grip of a struggle between democracy on one side and a monolithic communist empire on the other. The Nixon Doctrine, as his foreign policy came to be known, was based on the more mature view that world events were determined by a sophisticated interplay among several shifting centers of power that included not only the United States and Soviet Union, but also China, Japan, western Europe, and the emerging nations of the Third World.

The president on September 10, 1971.
PHOTO COURTESY NATIONAL ARCHIVES.

President Nixon meets in the Oval Office with three of his top aides,
National Security Adviser Henry Kissinger (left), John Ehrlichman
(center), and Bob Haldeman (right).
WHITE HOUSE PHOTO COURTESY *COURIER-EXPRESS* COLLECTION, E.H. BUTLER
LIBRARY, STATE UNIVERSITY COLLEGE AT BUFFALO AND BUFFALO AND ERIE
COUNTY HISTORICAL SOCIETY.

Since 1949, when the Communists had come to power in
China, the United States had used its influence to keep China
out of the United Nations. America and China did not have
diplomatic relations with each other and China was considered
a serious communist threat. In the eyes of the United States, it
was as though the world's most populous country did not even
exist, and Nixon recognized that such a situation could not
continue.

He sent his expert on national security and negotiator ex-
traordinaire, Henry Kissinger, to China for a series of secret
meetings that took place over a three year period. Kissinger's
work resulted in an invitation for Nixon to visit China early in
the winter of 1972.

The first family poses for a 1972 White House portrait. In rear, from left to right, are David Eisenhower, Julie Nixon Eisenhower, Tricia Nixon Cox, and Edward Cox. President and Mrs. Nixon are seated in front.

Along with a plane full of advisers and reporters, President Nixon arrived in the People's Republic of China and for a week conferred with China's great leaders, Mao Zedong and Zhou Enlai. He visited huge communal farms, ancient cities, and modern factories.

At the end of the trip, the Chinese and Americans issued a joint statement that became known as the Shanghai Communiqué, which outlined agreements "to expand cultural, educational, and journalist contacts between the Chinese and American people." Most important were agreements on certain rules of international conduct to reduce the risk of confrontation and war in Asia and the Pacific.

Nixon's tour of China was a triumph. "This was the week that changed the world," he said at a banquet with China's leaders at the end of the historic trip.

But even while the president was basking in his foreign policy success, the seeds of his political destruction were being sown. Members of his administration, high-ranking White House staffers, and even the attorney general, chief law enforcement officer of the United States, were secretly engaged in questionable activities, some of them considered unethical, others illegal.

Those activities first came to light on June 17, 1972, when five men, including the chief of security of the Committee to Re-elect the President (CREEP), were caught at the headquarters of the Democratic National Committee in the Watergate office building, arrested, and charged with burglary.

The *Washington Post* and other newspapers carried stories that claimed the burglary was linked to the White House, but Nixon and his aides denied any knowledge or complicity.

In fact, the White House blamed the press for blowing the story out of proportion, calling coverage of the break-in and subsequent investigations irresponsible, sensational journalism. Nixon ordered an investigation by his White House counsel, John Dean. But Dean himself would later be convicted for his role in covering up Watergate.

"I can say categorically that his investigation indicates that no one in the White House staff, no one in this administra-

Nixon, in February 1972, stands on the Great Wall of China during part of his history-making trip that marked the beginning of a new quest for peace with the world's largest nation.
PHOTO COURTESY NATIONAL ARCHIVES.

tion presently employed was involved in this bizarre incident," Nixon announced.

While the president's press secretary scornfully called the Watergate break-in a "third-rate burglary," others close to the president were arranging payoffs to the burglars so that they would quietly plead guilty and serve time in prison without implicating the White House. This "hush money" came from Nixon campaign funds, some of it illegally and secretly collected.

The cover-up worked at first. Even though George McGovern, Nixon's Democratic opponent for the presidency, and other Democrats tried to make Watergate an issue in the 1972 campaign, voters were reluctant to believe it was anything more than a political prank. In 1972, at the end of President Nixon's first term in office, Watergate was a tiny stone that was buried in his landslide reelection. On election day, Richard Nixon piled up a huge majority and took the electoral votes of every single state except Massachusetts and the District of Columbia.

10

The Light Fades

"We stand on the threshold of a new era of peace in the world," Nixon told Americans in his second inaugural address on January 20, 1973.

Even though it had taken over four years, the United States involvement in Vietnam was ending. Richard Nixon had brought about the impending end of the war by a steady withdrawal of American troops, which were gradually replaced by South Vietnamese soldiers; increased bombing and air support for the South Vietnamese; and negotiations with the North Vietnamese at the tedious and frustrating Paris peace talks.

Three days after his second inauguration, Nixon announced the agreement "to end the war and bring peace with honor," a pact that resulted in withdrawal of the last twenty-five thousand Americans there and release by the North Vietnamese of United States prisoners of war. A cease-fire began the day after the agreement was signed on January 27, 1973.

Nixon had followed up his trip to China with a summit conference in the Soviet Union. In Moscow, he made the first direct television speech by an American president to the Soviet people. "As great powers, we shall sometimes be competitors, but we need never be enemies."

The result of Nixon's visit was a distinct thaw in the "cold war" and the signing of nine different treaties and agreements, including a historic restriction on the development of nuclear weapons.

Nixon's visit was reciprocated in June of 1973 by Soviet leader Leonid I. Brezhnev who told the American people in his television address, that "a new spirit of cooperation and world peace" was developing.

All of his success, though, was being overshadowed by the dark clouds gathering on Richard Nixon's horizon. Despite the historic trip to China, the successful Moscow summit conference, the landslide reelection over George McGovern, and the end of the Vietnam War, the Nixon presidency had entered its final phase, the period of decline caused by Watergate.

The president works alone in the Oval Office. 1973.
PHOTO COURTESY NATIONAL ARCHIVES.

President Nixon answers questions at a 1973 White House press conference. During the last two years of his presidency, more and more press attention was focused on Watergate.
PHOTO COURTESY NATIONAL ARCHIVES.

Things started to unravel early in 1973 as more tantalizing information came to light and a pattern emerged. Judge John Sirica, who presided over the trials of the Watergate burglary defendants, was unhappy when they each pleaded guilty and refused to talk. He threatened them with maximum sentences up to forty years. Any of the burglars who would provide information would receive a lighter sentence, Sirica said.

One decided to testify before a Watergate grand jury. The press, especially two reporters at the *Washington Post*, Bob Woodward and Carl Bernstein, continued to investigate and print new revelations.

When the Senate set up the Watergate Committee, some of Nixon's aides added their accusations to a growing body of evidence. The House of Representatives Judiciary Committee discussed the possibility of a presidential impeachment for the first time in more than a century.

One shock followed another and evidence accumulated that Nixon and his top aides had made a list of enemies, tapped telephones, used illegal fund-raising techniques, authorized burglaries, cheated on taxes, and abused the power of the presidency by using agencies of the federal government, such as the FBI and Internal Revenue Service, to spy on and harass its "enemies."

Nixon's problems grew when Vice-President Spiro Agnew was forced to resign in October 1973 because he was about to be tried for accepting bribes, both while he was governor of Maryland and as vice-president.

As provided for under the recently ratified Twenty-Fifth Amendment to the Constitution, Nixon named the popular House of Representatives Minority Leader Gerald R. Ford to replace Agnew. Ford was quickly confirmed by the Senate and sworn in as the new vice-president.

As the Watergate story unfolded, Nixon tried to contain the political damage. At first he denied any link between the Watergate break-in and the White House. Later he claimed that although there had been some mistakes made, he, personally, had not known about them. When the existence of the Watergate tapes was revealed and investigators subpoenaed them, Nixon tried for more than a year to keep the conversations secret. He based his argument on "executive privilege," the right of an administration to keep discussions private. The issue went all the way to the Supreme Court.

Edited transcriptions of some tapes were released by the White House in an attempt to satisfy the growing public demand. Even though the first tapes released contained no hard evidence of any criminal responsibility on the part of the president, the *New York Times* said they "showed a president who was profane, indecisive, prolix, concerned more with saving his own skin than getting at the truth, and deeply involved in discussions about employing perjury and hush money to insulate himself from scandal." It was, according to the *Times*, "the most unflattering picture ever revealed of Richard Nixon."

After agonizing months of hearings and debate, the House Judiciary Committee wrote five articles of impeachment and

Nixon visits Rochester, New York, with his old Republican adversary, Nelson Rockefeller, on June 19, 1974. The visit was marred by angry demonstrations as his presidency was consumed by the Watergate scandal.
BUFFALO *COURIER-EXPRESS* PHOTO BY RIC DELANEY COURTESY E.H. BUTLER LIBRARY, STATE UNIVERSITY COLLEGE AT BUFFALO AND BUFFALO AND ERIE COUNTY HISTORICAL SOCIETY.

then voted in favor of three. The first charged that Nixon had personally conspired to "delay, impede, and obstruct the investigation" and "to cover up, conceal, and protect those responsible."

The president "has repeatedly engaged in conduct violating the constitutional rights of citizens," said the second. It also charged Nixon with "impairing the due and proper administration of justice."

The third article charged that the president had "willfully disobeyed" subpeonas for documents, tapes, and information. The two articles not approved by the committee dealt with Nixon's income taxes and the secret bombing of Cambodia.

Now the full House of Representatives would decide whether

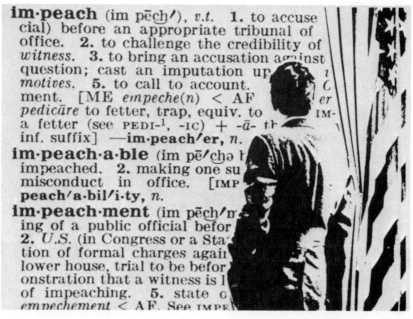

im·peach (im pēch/), *v.t.* **1.** to accuse
cial) before an appropriate tribunal of
office. **2.** to challenge the credibility of
witness. **3.** to bring an accusation a~~inst
question; cast an imputation up
motives. **5.** to call to account.
ment. [ME *empeche(n)* < AF
pedicāre to fetter, trap, equiv. to   IM-
a fetter (see PEDI-¹, -IC) + -ā- t.h
inf. suffix] —**im·peach/er,** *n.*
im·peach·a·ble (im pē/chə
impeached. **2.** making one su
misconduct in office. [IMP
peach/a·bil/i·ty, *n.*
im·peach·ment (im pēch/n
ing of a public official befor
2. *U.S.* (in Congress or a Sta
tion of formal charges agair
lower house, trial to be befor
onstration that a witness is l
of impeaching. **5.** state o
empechement < AF. See IMPE

Many American voices were calling for impeachment as the Watergate
scandal unfolded. This illustration appeared in the Buffalo *Courier-
Express* on February 24, 1974.

or not to impeach the president. Nixon hoped that his supporters in Congress would convince fellow representatives to vote
against impeachment and that, if the unthinkable should happen, he might not be found guilty in a trial by the Senate.

Those hopes crumpled, though, on July 24, 1974, when the
Supreme Court ruled unanimously that the tapes of sixty-four
White House conversations must be turned over to the Watergate prosecutors. Those tapes showed, among other things,
that Nixon had known about the Watergate break-in almost
immediately afterward and had been an active participant in the
cover-up.

Particularly damaging were three conversations on June 23,

President Nixon claims, in early May of 1974, that recently released transcripts of White House conversations will exonerate him and that old political enemies of his were responsible for fanning the fires of Watergate.

1972, five days after the break-in, when Nixon instructed Haldeman to tell the CIA that it should stop the FBI investigation into
the break-in. The CIA, Nixon said, should call in the FBI and tell
them "don't go any further into this case, period!"

Once the tapes were released, Nixon's presidency had no
chance to survive. In the ensuing storm, many of his loyal
supporters felt betrayed and turned against him. Impeachment
was certain and leaders of the Senate told the White House that
no more than ten Senators would be likely to vote against
conviction.

Nixon's only choice was to be convicted and forced out of
office, sacrificing his pension and other "perks" in the process,
or to resign. Only the members of his loyal and distraught
family were still urging him to fight on.

As the end of his presidency neared, Nixon had to name a new vice-
president and replace most of his senior staff. Here he meets in the
Oval Office with Secretary of State Henry Kissinger (left), Vice-Presi-
dent Gerald R. Ford (on Nixon's right), who replaced the fallen Spiro
Agnew, and Chief of Staff Alexander Haig (right), who replaced Bob
Haldeman. Only Kissinger had served Nixon from the beginning of his
presidency.
WHITE HOUSE PHOTO COURTESY *COURIER-EXPRESS* COLLECTION, E.H. BUTLER
LIBRARY, STATE UNIVERSITY COLLEGE AT BUFFALO AND BUFFALO AND ERIE
COUNTY HISTORICAL SOCIETY.

The president's family smiles bravely for a last White House picture
together, shortly after Nixon decided to resign.
PHOTO COURTESY NATIONAL ARCHIVES.

Julie Nixon Eisenhower wrote a heartfelt note to her father and
left it on his pillow. "Go through the fires a little longer," she
begged him. Julie believed in her father and she believed that the
country needed him. She could not accept what was about to
happen. But the loyalty of his family was all Nixon had left. The
pressure on him to resign was becoming overwhelming.

During those last few days in the White House, advisers faced
another agony, a sincere concern about Nixon's sanity. The
devastated president was growing increasingly depressed and
did not always appear rational. They tried to ease him into a
decision to resign. They feared direct pressure might send him
over the edge.

On Wednesday, August 7, Nixon met with a group of his

staunchest congressional supporters, who told him the situation was hopeless, and he finally seemed ready to accept their assessment. "I just wanted to hear it from you," he said.

After that meeting he told his family of his intention to resign. On Thursday morning he met with Vice-President Gerald Ford and informed him that he would become the new president the next day. "I have made the decision to resign," he told the vice-president. "It's in the best interest of the country. I won't go into the details pro and con. I have made my decision." He paused, then added, "Jerry, I know you'll do a good job."

Early that evening, Nixon met with forty of his most loyal supporters in the cabinet room. One congressman reported that he seemed like "a broken man." Nixon pulled himself together, however, and walked into the Oval Office to make his resignation speech to the nation.

Nixon's wife, Pat, and his two daughters waited upstairs in the family residence, devastated by what was about to happen. They had put on a brave front, but this was perhaps the worst moment of their lives. Julie Nixon Eisenhower had struggled to hide her tears as the family posed for a final White House portrait. They had all tried to look happy and strong, but Julie ducked behind her mother as her eyes brimmed with tears.

Vice-President Gerald Ford waited in his suburban Alexandria, Virginia, home, braced for the awesome responsibility that would soon fall onto his shoulders. Television cables snaked across his front lawn and the usually quiet street was snarled with traffic as reporters, neighbors, and the curiosity seekers waited and watched.

Henry Kissinger, secretary of state and a trusted Nixon adviser, listened to the speech outside the Oval Office. After it was over, he went into the office and approached the desk. The speech, he told Nixon in his deep, heavily accented voice, had "great dignity."

"I think we were all completely drained of emotion by the time he had spoken the last words," Julie Nixon Eisenhower wrote. "Wasn't it a great speech?" she asked a longtime family friend. "How did he do it?"

Bob Haldeman, who had once kept people from reaching the

president, tried to call, but this time he was the one who couldn't get through. He wanted to ask Nixon to pardon him and other Watergate figures, so they couldn't be prosecuted for crimes they may have committed. But there would be no pardon.

John Dean, the Watergate insider who had first broken rank and given damaging testimony to the Senate Watergate Committee, sat at home. He had already been tried for Watergate-related crimes, convicted, and would soon be going to prison. He listened to the speech and shook his head in amazement. "He never admitted a damn thing," Dean muttered. "He went out with a campaign speech. Why is he taking Watergate with him?"

"The speech lasted fifteen minutes, and at the end I was convinced that Nixon was out of touch with reality," Vice-President Gerald Ford later wrote in his autobiography. "If he had been more contrite and asked the American people for forgiveness, he would have received a warmer response. Yet he couldn't take that final step."

Nixon hadn't been ruthless enough, thought G. Gordon Liddy, one of the Watergate masterminds. He had listened to the speech from his sweltering cell in the ancient District of Columbia jail. Liddy thought Nixon should have destroyed the incriminating tapes. "Had he done so, he would have served out his term," Liddy said. "I had, at least, the knowledge that my silence had helped bring him more than two additional years as president." Liddy had steadfastly refused to testify and had been sent to the notorious District of Columbia jail for contempt of court instead of being sent to a less unpleasant federal prison like the others convicted of Watergate crimes.

Now the bitter Watergate saga drew to a close with the transition of presidential power from Richard M. Nixon to Gerald R. Ford. After his White House farewells, Nixon flew home to California, where he had been born and raised and where he had first pursued greatness and first suffered defeat.

He had faced defeat before and battled back against seemingly impossible odds. But this was different. This time it was over. No one expected another comeback.

Surrounded by his family, President Nixon bids an emotional farewell to the White House staff on his last morning as president, August 9, 1974.
PHOTO COURTESY NATIONAL ARCHIVES.

11

Another Beginning

The fallen president arrived at his San Clemente home in California with his wife, Pat, his daughter, Tricia, her husband, a few staff members, and Secret Service agents who would still protect him.

Even though there had been little time to pack, Pat Nixon had gathered some of her husband's favorite belongings so that his surroundings would seem more familiar and comfortable under the extraordinary circumstances.

When Nixon's plane landed at the Marine base near San Clemente, more than five thousand people were gathered there to greet him. A tired, ashen Nixon stepped off the plane and into the bright California sunshine. Someone began to sing "God Bless America." Other voices joined in and the patriotic music swelled into a stirring crescendo.

Nixon, moved, stopped briefly to speak to the crowd. "I am going to continue to work for peace among the world," he said. "I intend to continue to work for opportunity and understanding among the people in America."

It took time for Nixon to adjust to the change of pace at San Clemente. There were many little differences. The Marine guard in full-dress whites was gone from the front gate, replaced by a speaker system. The beach in front of his home, from which the Secret Service formerly kept the public, was now open to anyone who wanted to walk there. The vast communications system, which had once kept Nixon in instant touch with any point on the globe, was gradually dismantled.

Weeds began to sprout among the flowers on the once meticulous grounds. The grass grew a bit too tall. The formerly crowded staff parking lot was nearly empty.

Nixon spent his time resting and calling old friends. He was adjusting well, his press secretary told the world. But his family, friends, and staff were worried because he alternated between brief moments of euphoria and bouts of depression.

Nixon had many problems, not the least of them financial. He had massive legal bills to pay and, now that the federal government would no longer be caring for his estates, huge maintenance bills. He owed hundreds of thousands of dollars in back income taxes imposed when the IRS disallowed a deduction for the donation of his vice-presidential papers to the National Archives. His resources were dangerously low, his checking account balance dipping below five hundred dollars at one point.

Even more disturbing was the possibility that Nixon, now that he was a private citizen, might have to face criminal prosecution and perhaps jail as a result of Watergate.

Back in Washington, the Watergate prosecutor considered bringing formal charges against Nixon. Prosecutors in the trials of his former aides wanted him to testify. There was a strong possibility that the Watergate grand jury, which had already named Nixon as a coconspirator but had hesitated to indict a president, might do so now that he no longer held office.

Another worry was about Nixon's health. He had had several earlier bouts with phlebitis, a disease where blood clots form in the veins of the leg, causing painful swelling and the grave risk that a clot could break away from the leg and travel to the heart, which could cause death. The affected leg was sore and badly swollen. Nixon walked with a noticeable limp. He slept poorly and ate little. His friends and family worried.

Nixon's friends, including Alexander Haig, his most recent White House chief of staff and now an aide to President Ford, asked Ford to grant Nixon a pardon for any Watergate crimes he may have committed. Ford's staff was against a pardon, arguing that the American people were not ready to accept one.

Ford agonized. He knew his assistants were right when they said a pardon would be extremely unpopular. But he also believed that Nixon was a sick man who had suffered enough.

The pardon privilege is a right given presidents by the Constitution to officially forgive crimes. It is intended as one of the "checks and balances" to keep the branches of government working smoothly together. Pardon power means that the executive branch can overrule the judiciary. The writers of the Constitution believed that the power of a president to grant pardons would insure room for mercy in our justice system.

Gerald Ford decided that a pardon was necessary. "I was very sure of what would happen if I let the charges against Nixon run their legal course," Ford wrote in his autobiography. "Months were sure to elapse between indictment and trial. And Nixon could not spend time quietly in San Clemente. He would be fighting for his freedom, taking his cause to the people, and his constant struggle would have dominated the news.

"The story would overshadow everything else. No other issue could compete with the drama of a former president trying to stay out of jail. It would be virtually impossible for me to direct public attention to anything else. Passions on both sides would be aroused. A period of such prolonged vituperation and recrimination would be disastrous for the nation. America needed recovery, not revenge."

Once Ford had decided to pardon Nixon, he didn't want to wait. "To procrastinate, to agonize, and to wait for a more favorable turn of events is a weak and potentially dangerous course for a president to follow."

On Sunday morning, September 8, 1974, President Ford announced a pardon of Richard Nixon for "all offenses against the United States which he, Richard Nixon, has committed or may have committed or taken part in during the period from January 20, 1969, through August 9, 1974."

Nixon had never admitted to any criminal conduct, so accepting the pardon was humiliating for him.

The pardon caused Ford's popularity to take a sharp dive in the polls. Thousands of letters and telegrams deluged the White House.

The public anger disturbed Nixon, who called Ford and apologized. He offered to give back the pardon if it would help, but Ford brusquely refused. Nixon's despair deepened and his health grew worse.

While he was visiting a friend in Palm Springs, California, the phlebitis flared up. Nixon's doctor was summoned. He wanted to send Nixon to the hospital, but Nixon refused to go. "If I go to the hospital, I'll never get out of there alive," he told the doctor.

Mrs. Nixon, gravely concerned, called a second doctor in Washington, who rushed to California, examined the former president, and also tried to get him to accept hospital treatment. Nixon finally agreed to go, but many Americans claimed that he was faking illness as an excuse to avoid testifying in the trials of John Mitchell, Bob Haldeman, and John Ehrlichman.

Nixon was given tests in the hospital, then released to continue his recovery at home. Powerful drugs were administered to thin his blood and dissolve the clot. But by late October the swelling had not subsided, and he was taken to the hospital again, this time for surgery. The operation went smoothly and Nixon was taken back to his room.

That afternoon a nurse discovered him unconscious. "Richard, Richard," she shouted at him as she slapped his face. He didn't revive. He had gone into shock caused by internal bleeding. For three hours a medical team fought to save his life.

The former president pulled through, but remained in critical condition for more than a week, and hospitalized for another week after that. It had been a close call.

Later, when he was feeling better, Nixon remembered the lapse into shock and the nurse shouting, "Richard, pull yourself back. Pull yourself back." He had felt himself facing a choice. He could give up and slip into oblivion or he could go on. At that instant, he decided to go on. There was more for him to do. It was not yet time for his life to end. His condition stabilized and his long recovery began.

He returned to San Clemente to regain strength and to work on a book of memoirs, for which he would be paid more than $2.5 million, funds he desperately needed to pay mounting legal fees, hospital bills, and taxes.

Early in the new year came the devastating news that a jury had found Haldeman, Mitchell, and Ehrlichman guilty. Each was given a prison sentence of up to three years.

Nixon stayed in seclusion in San Clemente. Later that year he sold a series of four exclusive ninety-minute television interviews to David Frost, a British television personality, for six hundred thousand dollars plus 20 percent of the profits. The interviews attracted large audiences, although nothing new or significant emerged. The Frost interviews helped to ease Nixon's continuing financial difficulties.

After more than a year of exile, Nixon began to emerge from isolation. The leaders of China had stayed in touch with the former president, whom they considered a great leader. They sent him frequent invitations to visit, so Nixon decided to travel to China in February of 1976.

Nixon's memoirs were finally published in 1978 and immediately became a best-selling book despite some critical reviews. Then, in 1980, Nixon decided to move back to New York.

After a year in Manhattan he moved again, to nearby Saddle River, New Jersey. He spent several days a week in his suite of offices in the Federal Plaza office building in New York, and he continued to write books that always sold well.

Shortly after Ronald Reagan became president, Anwar Sadat, Egypt's president and an important American ally, was assassinated. Reagan wanted to express the respect of the American people in a fitting way, but he and his advisers decided it was far too dangerous for the president or vice-president to travel to Cairo for the funeral.

Instead, Reagan asked the three living former presidents, Richard Nixon, Gerald Ford, and Jimmy Carter, to make the trip in his stead. The three men agreed and traveled together to Egypt aboard the presidential jetliner, Air Force One. The atmosphere was strained at first, but Ford broke the ice.

"Look, for this trip, at least, why don't we make it just Dick,

Jimmy, and Jerry," he said. Nixon and Carter agreed and the rest of the flight went smoothly. Afterward Nixon traveled on to visit leaders of several other countries in the Middle East.

After the former president's return home, Ronald Reagan became a frequent telephone caller, seeking Nixon's advice on a variety of subjects, especially foreign policy. Nixon continued to travel abroad, where he was still welcomed by world leaders and consulted about world events.

By the time he celebrated his seventy-fifth birthday on January 9, 1988, he had once again become a man whose opinions were sought and respected. His seventh book, *1999: Victory Without War*, immediately reached the best-seller lists and Nixon found himself in demand as a television talk show guest and as a counselor to many Republican candidates who journeyed to Saddle River to ask his advice.

Even a few Democrats began taking Richard Nixon seriously again. New York Governor Mario Cuomo suggested that Nixon's experience be put to use on behalf of his country as a negotiator for nuclear disarmament.

The former president is closer to his family than ever before. "Pat and our daughters have been my tower of strength, both in good times and bad," he said. "Julie and Tricia have given me four wonderful grandchildren, and it's a delight to watch them grow up."

The children call the former president "Ba" and their grandmother "Ma." Mrs. Nixon, who has suffered several mild strokes, stays out of the public spotlight, devoting most of her time to her family and especially to activities with her grandchildren.

Richard Nixon is in better health, thanks to the long walks he regularly takes and the fact that he is finally learning to relax. "He's seventy-five, going on fifty," says David Eisenhower.

Richard Nixon is mellower now, at peace with himself and his family, tempered by the fires he's been through. He's still waging a political battle, but not for voter approval. He's not struggling with Congress nor with the courts. This time he's fighting for his place in history.

"History will treat me fairly," he said in an April 1988 inter-

Three presidents wait to pay their last respects to Hubert H. Humphrey at the nation's Capitol on January 15, 1978. Former Presidents Richard Nixon and Gerald R. Ford talk quietly with President Jimmy Carter while they wait to attend the Humphrey funeral.
PHOTO COURTESY JIMMY CARTER LIBRARY.

view on NBC-TVs "Meet the Press." "We changed the world. If it had not been for the China initiative, which only I could do at that point, we would be in a terrible situation today, with China aligned with the Soviet Union and with the Soviet Union's power. The China initiative hasn't brought peace to the world. We can't be sure that will happen. But without it we would be in terrible shape."

The former president admitted that "Watergate was a breach of trust" and described how Winston Churchill had once written that strong leaders usually handle big things well but foul up on small things, which then get big. "I should have read that before Watergate happened. In 1972 we went to China. We went to Russia. We ended the Vietnam War effectively by the end of that year. Those were the big things. And here was a small

Former Presidents Nixon and Ford with Lady Bird Johnson, former first lady and the widow of Lyndon Johnson, at the funeral of Hubert H. Humphrey, Johnson's vice-president and Richard Nixon's 1968 opponent for the presidency, January 15, 1978.
PHOTO COURTESY JIMMY CARTER LIBRARY.

thing, and we fouled it up beyond belief. It was a great mistake. It was wrong."

Richard Nixon then offered this advice to future leaders: "Do the big things as well as you can, but when a small thing is there, deal with it, and deal with it fast. Get it out of the way, because if you don't, it's going to become big, and then it may destroy you."

In December 1988 ground was broken for the Richard M. Nixon Presidential Library on a site next-door to Nixon's birthplace in Yorba Linda, California. The privately funded $25 million center, scheduled to open in 1990, will house a museum, theater, exhibit hall, offices, and document storage area. The famous Watergate tapes won't be there, however. Neither will Nixon's presidential papers. Courts have ruled that they are the property of the American public and have given custody to the National Archives, which keeps them at a facility open to the public in suburban Washington, D.C.

Ground-breaking ceremonies for Nixon's private library attracted more than one thousand dignitaries and friends of the former president, including his former chief of staff, H. R. Haldeman, one of the convicted Watergate figures. Speakers included Henry Kissinger, Nixon's secretary of state, who praised President Nixon's vital role in creating better relations with the Soviet Union and the People's Republic of China, and Julie Nixon Eisenhower, who said she hopes the new library will provide help for Americans to evaluate her father's administration in a new light and "help tear down some of the stereotypes."

The answer to the question about what kind of a president Richard Milhous Nixon really was will have to wait, according to Julie. "Only history can be the judge," she said.

Index